# Epic Train Journeys

*The Inside Track to the World's Greatest Rail Routes*

*Monisha Rajesh*

gestalten

# All Aboard for a Whistle-Stop Tour of the World

*Whether fast or slow, steam or electric, a journey by train sparks a special kind of romance for the cast of characters, changing scenery, and wonderful food on board.*

By Monisha Rajesh

Perched on the top of the steps, tea in hand, I listened to the wheels clanking and turned my face toward the sun. With warm wind came the smell of burning fields. An ox cart rumbled alongside, so slow was our pace, its owner bobbing on a stack of sugarcane. Looping one arm around the handhold, I shuffled up as a fellow passenger joined me in the open doorway and leaned out toward the soft evening light. Together we sat in silence, no sound but the beat of the train. There are few places where I feel at peace, but that top step is one of them. Indian trains are famed for traveling with the doors latched open, a breeze sailing through, and passengers hopping on and off at will. Rolling through the countryside as a setting sun unfurls pink ribbons across the sky, I am filled with a sense of place and purpose, bearing witness to the world as it passes by.

In 2010, I set off on a four-month journey around India. With no interest in trains, no railroading family, no nostalgic tales of riding the rails as a kid, I chose to see the country with a rail pass because it was cheap, and it brought me into contact with people I would otherwise never have met. In between journeys, I would spend time in sleepy towns and raging cities, exploring mostly on foot, but reboarding those trains soon felt like coming home: the familiarity of the beat as we moved off, the clatter of acceleration, the warm breeze blowing in from outside. I had never expected to find an affinity for the railways, let alone one that took hold so fast. The railways are a microcosm of society, with the wealthiest at one end, the poorest at the other, and everyone else in between. In a single journey, I could draw out stories from politicians, businessmen, and teachers, then sway down the aisles to squat on wooden slats talking to laborers and elderly men selling fruit. But before long, I realized that the railways themselves had become the main protagonist of my story, and a love affair with trains began to bloom. Traveling on express trains, steam trains, Mumbai's infamous commuter trains, and even a hospital on wheels, I came to understand why Indian Railways is known as the lifeline of a nation that keeps the country's heart beating.

Soon after my journey ended, naysayers began to sound the death knell for long-distance services in the face of bullet trains and budget airlines. Too long, too old, too expensive, they said. But I knew in my heart they were wrong. After my Indian adventure, I found myself drawn to trains wherever I traveled, seeking out routes and wandering around stations. At night, I would lie in bed listening to the distant horn of a passing train and pause on bridges watching them thunder below. The urge →

Above: The Boat Mail or Indo-Ceylon Express traveling from Rameswaram to Chennai-Egmore in Southeast India, crosses the Pamban Bridge.

Right page: A regular commuter service bound for Nice curls around the Anthéor Viaduct in Saint-Raphaël, France.

In the United States, Amtrak's observation cars (pictured below left) offer passengers a trackside view of the vast American landscape. Known as sightseer lounges, these are available on long-distance trains only, bringing together a cast of characters for the ride. Filled on a first-come, first-served basis, they are the heart of all the action.

7

→ to travel was so overwhelming that five years after my journey around India, I packed my bags yet again and set off in the hope of rediscovering the romance of the railways, this time on a transcontinental journey through Europe, Asia, and North America. After seven months and 45,000 miles (72,420 kilometers), I returned triumphant, having witnessed how people everywhere will always need those services, no matter how old, how battered, or how remote. Spread out a map, and you will see blood-red arteries rippling across the land, thinning into the furthest corners. Winding up mountains, skimming coasts, and crossing borders, these networks offer employment to some, joy to others, and a lifeline to everyone else. Whether you are traveling from Shanghai to Beijing, New York to New Orleans, or Moscow to Berlin, there is a wonderful train that can make that journey. While on board, you will find that countries and people open up in a way that is specific to train travel.

Your sense of time and space become clearer and sharper as you pass between villages, cities, and states, rivers weaving and mountains rising like markers along the way. From the window you see borders appear then recede, languages change on signs, currency change in your hands. It is an intimacy unique to railways, one that binds us together. To date, trains remain my preferred method of travel, whether it is a short hop to visit friends around England or a family vacation within Europe. And the sound of a train's whistle will forever be my call to prayer.

Throughout this book, there are a variety of routes to satisfy your curiosity, budget, and wanderlust. It is perfectly possible to trundle →

→ through the Scottish Highlands sipping single malt under a tartan duvet—or make the same journey with a jacket for a pillow and a piece of shortbread for breakfast. There are trains that ascend into the Peruvian clouds, trains that roll by the Pacific Ocean, and trains that clatter along routes built by prisoners of war. Propped up in bed with a cup of frothy coffee, you are granted the luxury of going nowhere, while going everywhere, with a front-row ticket to the theatre of Vietnam's villages in the morning, Australia's outback at sunset, and the extraordinary first sights of Siberia's lakes or Canada's snow-capped Rockies. Do not assume, though, that the longer the journey the better; in just a few hours you could wind through the American South, crawl down the middle of a Thai market selling crabs, or chug against the wind on the Patagonian steppe. There are week-long luxury trains that hark back to a bygone era, with liveried staff and diners in black tie. But there are also magnificent trains serving commuters, long immune to the splendor of their local scenery. Owing to the lack of modernization in infrastructure in South and Central America, and parts of Africa where railroads are isolated in the absence of an expansive network, the majority of the routes here center on Europe, Asia, and North America, with a handful of outstanding journeys dotted around the globe.

It could be argued that flying is quicker and often cheaper, but with the ever-growing threat of climate change and a push toward slow travel, airplanes are fast becoming the villain in the story. And who wants to waste time removing shoes, unbuckling belts, collapsing buggies, forgetting iPads, emptying bottles, and enduring all manner of pats, pokes, and scans, when by train you stay clothed, untouched, and unhurried—with as many bottles as you like? There are no hidden charges for wider seats, excess luggage, or early boarding, and increasingly there is digital connectivity, making it easy to send emails, make phone calls, and finish work, before winding down with dinner and a good book. Sleeper trains are like arrows,

firing straight into the heart of a city. They will not leave you on the peripheries, battling taxi queues with bleary-eyed annoyance, but will carry you in alongside fields thawing in first light, tea vats bubbling on pavements, and wet-haired schoolkids waiting for the bus—dropping you right where you need to be.

This book introduces some of the highest, fastest, longest, and most historic trains in the world, allowing you to rediscover not just a magical mode of travel, but cities and spaces you may never have seen before—including North Korea. Along the way, you will find tips on packing for an overnight trip, the art of striking up conversation with fellow passengers, and how to stay sane on a four-night journey. The truth is, we all love a good train ride, and everyone has a favorite story to tell. Whether it is of vodka sessions on the Trans-Siberian with raucous Russian soldiers, or Tibetan nuns with gold iPhones, these tales are imbued with energy and spirit, and more often than not the kindness of strangers. Within the four walls of a train compartment, friendships ignite, politics are discussed, stories are shared, and books are swapped. Once on board, you are part of a family, a motley crew of characters brought together by chance and circumstance. And throughout that time, a certain trust extends between you, one that allows you to guard each other's luggage, exchange snacks, and keep each other's secrets. And so, in keeping with the best adventures, I invite you to make a cup of tea, sit back, and enjoy the ride. ♦

A luxury journey with South Africa's Rovos Rail can be designed to include visits to private game reserves where passengers have the chance to see the Big Five, as well as numerous other species including cheetah, giraffe, hippo, hyena, springbok, and gazelle.

# Bernina Express

*The highest railway across the Alps curves around glistening glaciers and roaring rivers toward sun-dappled meadows and pretty Italian towns.*

FROM CHUR, SWITZERLAND TO TIRANO, ITALY

4 HOURS

Slow, but steady, this sleek train takes just over four hours to weave its way between Chur in Switzerland and Tirano in Italy. More than a hundred years old, the Bernina Express route includes 55 tunnels and 196 bridges, offering passengers an extraordinary Alpine adventure—all from within the warm confines of a panoramic dome car. In winter, sunshine flashes through the windows, ricocheting off crisp white snow and ice-blue lakes. And in summer, bell-wearing cows graze knee-deep in meadows, picking their way through carpets of purple asters surrounded by snow-capped peaks.

The journey can feel precarious at times, as the train crosses bridges whose pillars are anchored in vertical rock faces, while milky rivers tumble below. But it is all part of the experience, and the train soon emerges from echoing tunnels into valleys dotted with bright terra-cotta roofs, neat wooden churches, and picket fences. A photographer's dream, the route is famous for the Landwasser Viaduct at Filisur, a single-track, six-arched limestone viaduct that takes you skirting above a 213-foot (65-meter) drop and directly into a tunnel built through a sheer rock wall. Consider adding to the adventure with an overnight stay in the medieval town of Poschiavo. If you time it correctly, you can browse the Wednesday market for some local burrata and wine, hike around the lake, then finish the day with a hearty dinner at Hostaria del Borgo, which does wonderful *osso buco*. Reboard the following day for the final 45-minute stretch to Tirano. ♦

*Point of interest:*
the Landwasser Viaduct

*Make sure to:*
*pack lunch as there*
*is a roving minibar*
*only and no restaurant*
*car on board*

Wonderful all year round, the
Bernina Express is particularly
beautiful in winter: under bright,
clear skies, the train takes
passengers around snow-covered
peaks, frozen rivers, and lakes
that glisten like glass.

# The Rauma Railway

*Short but impactful, this service showcases the best of Norway's mountains, rivers, and lakes, passing through six tunnels and 32 bridges en route.*

FROM ÅNDALSNES TO DOMBÅS, NORWAY
1 HOUR 40 MINUTES

Construction of the Rauma line began in 1912 in the village of Dombås and was completed in stages until the entire line was opened in November 1924 by King Haakon VII. Although intended to be a branch-line commuter service, the train has adopted several guises in its time, moonlighting as a transporter of the Bank of Norway's gold reserves during the Second World War and serving as a night mail carrier.

Now it is quite unashamedly a tourist train, whose sole purpose is to present Norway at its most wild and raw, carrying passengers alongside towering mountains, and over rivers thrashing below bridges. With a glossy brochure and route map distributed on board—along with audio commentaries in Norwegian, English, and German—the train is one of the best ways to pass 90 minutes in the country's northwest. Neither terminus is wildly exciting; however, the journey is your destination. Departing Åndalsnes four times a day, the train quickly leaves the grit of the town behind as it sails by picket-fenced meadows carpeted with buttercups and daisies. Brooks babble trackside, and small houses dot around the slopes. But this gentle and relaxing scenery swiftly morphs into mountain territory, where vertical peaks wear scarves of cloud, and gravelly grey tongues stretch down their sides where glaciers once moved. The Rauma River tumbles and bubbles over boulders, foaming as though filled with soap. Creamy sandbanks rise up from turquoise water, and lone salmon fishermen stand knee-deep in the swirl. Stopping at key spots along the way, the train offers plenty of opportunities for photographers to get their shots and for others to simply stop and breathe in the beauty. ♦

*Point of interest:*
*the Kylling bridge near*
*the village of Verma*

*Make sure to:*
*hop off at Bjorli if you're*
*traveling in winter—the*
*off-piste skiing is excellent*

Trundling through mountainous
territory, over sheer drops down
to tumbling rivers, the train
provides passengers with more
than a few opportunities to
photograph Norway in all its
natural beauty.

Known commonly as the Northern Lights, the natural phenomenon of *aurora borealis* occurs most frequently from September to late March, between 6:00 p.m. and 1:00 a.m., climaxing when the weather is cold and dry.

# Stockholm to Narvik

*Many European sleeper services have been retired in the face of high-speed rail, but this popular route takes passengers into the Arctic Circle.*

FROM STOCKHOLM, SWEDEN TO NARVIK, NORWAY
19 HOURS

One of Europe's most spectacular night trains, the direct sleeper service from Sweden to Norway is a fun and easy way to travel north into the Arctic Circle. At the time of writing, one direct train departs Stockholm Central each evening and arrives in Narvik 19 hours later, giving passengers plenty of time to enjoy the scenery at each end of the journey—with a decent night's sleep in between. A favorite of large families and sporty types heading north for some backcountry skiing, the train offers six-person or three-person compartments with access to a communal shower and toilet. For those preferring to travel with a little more privacy, you can book a first-class compartment, which comes with only two berths and an en suite shower and toilet. When you wake, make your way to the bistro car for a coffee and a breakfast box, where you can watch the terrain whip by—a dramatic expanse of lakes, forests, and tiny towns.

Keep in mind that if you travel in winter, you will experience less than six hours of daylight but have a high chance of seeing the Northern Lights: neon green beams dancing across the star-spattered skies like nature's own laser show. However, from May to July, you will have the benefit of the midnight sun, when the fjords and surrounding mountains are soaked in rich oranges and reds. On arrival in Narvik, there is the opportunity for late-night hikes or fishing on the lakes, where you will find plenty of locals making the most of the 24-hour light. ♦

# Jazz Night Express

*Dance the night away on board this mobile jazz club, featuring singers, DJs, and a Cajun kitchen on wheels.*

FROM ROTTERDAM, NETHERLANDS
TO BERLIN, GERMANY
12.5 HOURS

Night trains conjure up a special kind of magic: cozy berths, mysterious passengers, and the world whipping by in the darkness. Add to that some dinner, drinks, and dancing, and you have an all-night party on your hands. Taking place every July, the Jazz Night Express is the brainchild of Chris Engelsman, an engineer with a passion for trains. Despairing at the cutbacks to European overnight services, he and a couple of fellow train aficionados collaborated to showcase the joy of night-train travel.

The team rented rolling stock and then hired jazz musicians to tie in with the rhythm of the train. With three stages—one at each end and one in the middle to relieve crowding—the train features a mix of new talent, established performers, and DJs playing to travelers aged between four and 83 years old. Departing at sunset, the train plunges through the Dutch countryside, taking just over 12 hours to wind east as passengers sway to the blues and delight in Cajun-style meatloaf, shrimp jambalaya, and apple crumb cake. With capacity for 400 passengers, the train features comfortable couchettes with five sleeping places per compartment, and bed linens are provided. Luxury sleeping carriages house three beds per compartment, with air-conditioning, a seating corner, and a private washstand. Although the music is supposed to wind down by midnight, the party can carry on until 6:00 a.m. with a twirl or two on passing platforms before the train pulls into Berlin's Zoologischer Garten Station at 8:00 a.m. ◆

In homage to the unique joy of night-train travel, the journey includes all the ingredients for an overnight adventure: scenery, music, food and drink, and wonderful company.

With capacity for 400 passengers, there are no age restrictions on board the Jazz Night Express: travelers range from four to 83 years old and come from all over the world.

*Point of interest:*
live music taking place
at three different stages
on board

*Make sure to:*
check out the breakfast
club from 7:00 a.m.

# Le Petit Train Jaune

*Skirting the Spanish border, this colorful French train trundles around some of the Pyrenees' most beautiful landscapes.*

FROM LATOUR-DE-CAROL
TO VILLEFRANCHE-DE-CONFLENT, FRANCE
3 HOURS

Canary-yellow with red piping, this little train looks like a character from a children's storybook. Known officially as the Ligne de Cerdagne, the narrow-gauge railroad was built between 1903 and 1927 to link the Catalan plateau with the rest of the region. Hooting in and out of 19 tunnels and clattering over two extraordinary bridges, the train covers 39 miles (63 kilometers) of fabulous engineering work in just under three hours. With both closed and open-air carriages, the electric train gives passengers the chance to ride through the Pyrenees with the mountain wind whipping through their hair. Departing throughout the year, the train offers two very different experiences between summer and winter: in warmer months you will rumble by sweet-smelling meadows and yellow slopes, where gentians bloom like an orchestra of tiny blue trumpets, and butterflies flit overhead. Rivers gurgle through the trees and hikers wave from the trails. But winter brings a bright white blanket of snow, with naked trees shivering in the cold. In keeping with the rustic charm of the surrounding area, passengers are free to flag down the train as it passes, clambering into any available space before it gives a comical "poop-poop," rattles, then revs off. Hugging rock faces and skirting canyons, the train reaches the highlight of the journey at the Pont Gisclard—unless you suffer from a fear of heights, in which case you might want to close your eyes as the train crosses the suspension bridge above a deep valley of evergreen trees. ♦

During the summer months, passengers can travel along the route in open-air carriages, guaranteeing an opportunity for spectacular photographs of the Pyrenees and their surrounding scenery.

*Point of interest:*
Bolquère-Eyne is the highest
SNCF station in France

*Make sure to:*
arrive at least half an hour
before departure to ensure
you get a good seat

# The French Riviera Railway

*There is no glitz or glamor on board this commuter train that curves around the Côte d'Azur, revealing the region's best-kept secrets.*

| FROM FRÉJUS, FRANCE TO VENTIMIGLIA, ITALY
| 3 HOURS

Fast and functional, the regional express train that runs along this route from France into Italy begins in the historic town of Fréjus, and ends three hours later in the lovely Italian market town of Ventimiglia. Following the edge of the sparkling Ligurian sea, the double-decker train is akin to a bus service taking surly teens to school, waitresses to work, and carefully coiffed ladies to the beach with their dogs. Upstairs you will find graffiti in *verlan,* marker on the windows, and young couples getting overfamiliar, but it is the best place to sit to feel the warmth of the Mediterranean sunshine, absorb views of the ocean—and peek into people's houses. Stopping at major stations including Cannes, Nice, and Monaco, the train also threads into lesser-known coastal hideaways such as Cagnes-sur-Mer, Juan-les-Pins, and Antibes, where passengers should consider breaking the journey for a slice of fishy *pissaladière* and a stroll around the town. Here the beaches are much quieter, the water cleaner, and restaurants less crowded. When the sea disappears behind buildings, sit on the left-hand side, and scan the sun-kissed villages where bougainvillea pour down the walls of pink apartment blocks, and men with hairy orange chests play *pétanque.* As the train draws into Nice and Monaco, it brings passengers within gawking distance of magnificent yachts bobbing in the bays, tanned students playing beach volleyball, and Lamborghinis growling along the streets. Roughly stacked hillsides soon loom into view, and the train begins to sail into the old Italian station. ♦

# The Cinque Terre Railway

*Dotted along the rugged cliffs of Italy's Ligurian coast, this string of pastel-colored villages is most accessible by the regular commuter train.*

FROM LA SPEZIA TO LEVANTO, ITALY
29 MINUTES

One of Italy's most popular regions, the Cinque Terre fulfills every fantasy about the country. Built on the rocky coastline, this group of five fishing villages features medieval cobbles, friendly hotels, and family-run *trattorie*. In between the villages, you can find hidden shrines and chapels, terraced vineyards, and old footpaths flanked by olive groves. Visitors typically hike the trails connecting Monterosso, Vernazza, Corniglia, Manarola, and Riomaggiore—each of which takes a couple of hours—but the four-minute bursts by train between the villages offer a peek into parts you are unlikely to see on foot. Disappearing in and out of hillside tunnels, the train hugs the precipice of this gelato-colored jumble of villages while the sea sloshes against the rocks below. From the window, passengers are treated to the sight of flat-capped farmers tending their allotments, resident cats tight-rope walking on crumbling orange walls, and sudden bursts of soft-pink cherry blossom. Although trains run regularly throughout the day, the best service to take is the slowest regional train, which will add on little more than 10 minutes to the 20-minute journey, and allows passengers to listen out for the sound of church bells carrying through the trees, and to smell the scent of lemon and rosemary, heavy in the warm air. Buying a Cinque Terre Train Card means you can hop off in one village to enjoy a wood-fired pizza and a stroll around the town, then board the next train onward. ♦

*Points of interest:*
*ocean views*

*Make sure to:*
*buy the Cinque Terre Train*
*Card which includes unlimited*
*day train travel and access*
*to all hiking trails*

As the train winds its way around
the coastline, keep an eye out
for the lovely sight of multicolored
pastel houses cascading down
the hillside, with laundry drying
on balconies and lights glowing
through the shutters.

Normally the kind of train to attract foreign tourists only, the Douro Valley line is a national favorite visited by local families and Portuguese travelers who enjoy a sweet tipple on the move.

# The Douro Valley Railway

*Not short of picturesque train routes and charming stations, Portugal is home to one of the sweetest train rides in Europe—literally.*

FROM RÉGUA TO RÉGUA, PORTUGAL
3 HOURS

If you have never been to Portugal, one of the smartest ways to get to know the country and its culture is via the slow trains. Weaving through wine country, connecting major cities, and traveling to the edges of the coastline, the trains offer a fun way to meet local people and explore the places behind Portugal's most famous product: port wine. One celebrated train that focuses on the latter is the historic Douro Valley line that embarks on a riverside round-trip for those who fancy a tipple on the move. Built in 1925, the steam train with its five wooden carriages is something of a national treasure that attracts local riders and oenophiles, as well as curious tourists. With polished wooden benches and the windows thrown wide open, the train emits a long, loud hiss then puffs its way out of Régua station, leaving a trail of black smoke in its wake. On a bright day, there is no better way to spend three hours than following the bends of the wide-mouthed Douro River through the sun-dappled valley, a patchwork quilt of traditional terraced vineyards, *quintas,* and olive trees. Throughout the journey, local musicians bang tambourines, strum guitars, and squeeze accordions while passengers sip from glasses of sweet Ferreira port and clutch paper bags of *rebuçados da Régua*— hard, honeyed candies sold by ladies in white smocks. Its whistle piercing the tranquil air, the train passes through Pinhão and Tua stations, where passengers can hop out to stretch their legs and buy a couple of bottles of port to take home. Traveling full circle, the train returns to Régua with a final hiss and creak. ♦

*Point of interest:*
*Pinhão Train Station, which is*
*decorated with tiled blue mosaics*
*and has a wine shop on-site*

*Make sure to:*
*buy a bag of candies from*
*the ladies on the platform*

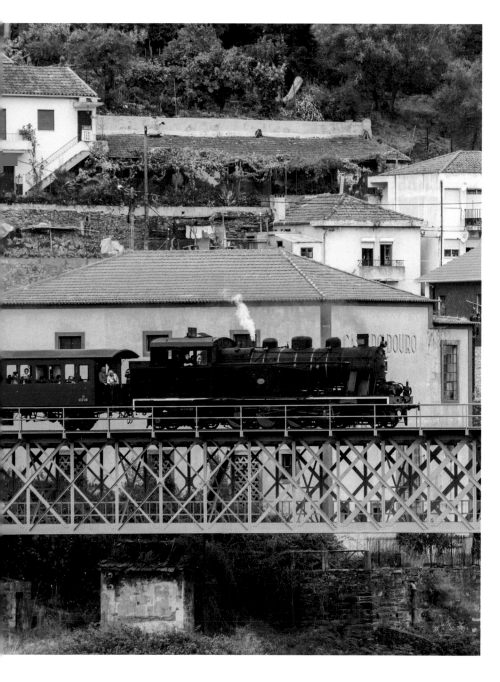

Left: Pinhão Train Station is worth a visit even if you are not traveling on the train. Its whitewashed walls are decorated with traditional glazed blue tiles known as *azulejos*, many of which portray historic scenes of the region.

45

# The Caledonian Sleeper

*In 2019, the storied history of this well-loved service began a fresh chapter when a fleet of brand new trains were introduced between London and Scotland.*

FROM LONDON, ENGLAND TO INVERNESS, SCOTLAND
11.5 HOURS

An old favorite of journalists, musicians, and politicians commuting to London for work, the Caledonian Sleeper is one of only two night services left in the U.K., the other being the Night Riviera from London to Penzance, Cornwall. Connecting London with Edinburgh and Glasgow on the Lowlander route—and Aberdeen, Fort William, and Inverness on the Highlander route—the train is a stress-free way to travel through the night and arrive fresh for the day ahead. Various versions of the Caledonian Sleeper have been in almost continuous operation since 1873, but a recent $200m refurbishment has breathed life into what had become a creaky, shabby old service. Spruced up to feature double beds with Glencraft mattresses, and en suite bathrooms with showers and luxury toiletries, the train is now more of a mobile bed-and-breakfast than a mode of transport. Along with the interiors, the menu has seen a grand overhaul, so make your way to the dining car and get into the spirit of things with a platter of hot smoked salmon, followed by traditional haggis, neeps and tatties served with whiskey cream sauce. Knock back a wee dram in the lounge car then drift off as London falls away in the dark, raising the blinds at dawn to the morning mists above the moors. The cultural capital of the Highlands, Inverness, is a stone's throw from Loch Ness and an ideal hub from which to explore the country's wildest beauty. ◆

# The West Highland Line

*With magical views of mountains, lochs, and sweeping glens, this Scottish adventure finds beauty at every twist and turn.*

FROM GLASGOW TO MALLAIG, SCOTLAND
5.5 HOURS

When Glasgow Queen Street Station's ugly 1960s façade was recently demolished, it was mourned by no one. A fashionable new glass-fronted facelift may not be to everyone's taste, but it is certainly an upgrade for passengers embarking upon the West Highland line to Mallaig.

After pulling out of the city center, the train follows the River Clyde northwest before swinging into the countryside and plunging passengers into a Scottish wilderness free from roads, cars, and people. Surrounded by valleys mottled with the purple of wild heather, the train soon curves up and around the bonny banks of Loch Lomond, clinging to hillsides lined with birch trees. Not long after Tyndrum, the train performs a twist around the horseshoe bend at the foot of Beinn Dorain before continuing up to Fort William. It is a glorious ride in summer, but if you are willing to brave the brisk winds and sleet, a winter excursion will add an extra layer of beauty in the form of frosted rivers and icicles dangling from trees.

From Fort William, the track veers off into the wilderness with place names becoming more commonly Gaelic as the train rumbles west. Here you might be lucky enough to witness the sun descend on the Inner Hebrides: a rare moment when the water shimmers purple and pink. From Mallaig, a 45-minute ferry service carries you over to the mighty Isle of Skye. Few British islands capture the spirit of nature quite like this one, where golden eagles soar on the wind, herds of red deer gather on the glens, and the granite monolith known as the Old Man of Storr stands guard like an ancient protector. ♦

*Point of interest:*
*the Glenfinnan Viaduct,*
*which overlooks Loch Shiel,*
*was made famous by the*
*Harry Potter movie franchise*

*Make sure to:*
*keep your eyes peeled for*
*deer and other wildlife*

The train journey highlights much
of Scotland's rugged and natural
beauty, but it is also worth bringing
along a pair of binoculars to spot
wildlife in the form of golden
eagles and roe deer.

# Belmond Royal Scotsman

*Kick back and enjoy a luxurious journey through the rolling mountains of the Scottish Highlands, with five-star dining and no expense spared.*

FROM EDINBURGH TO EDINBURGH, SCOTLAND
7 NIGHTS

Over seven nights with 24-hour steward service, four-course dinners, and many, many whiskies, a trip on the Belmond Royal Scotsman presents a rare opportunity to savor Scotland in all its glory.

Boarding in Edinburgh onto what feels like a very long and narrow Edwardian country house, you will be shown to a private compartment complete with tartan cushions, lacquer-polished wood paneling, and bright tufts of fresh heather on the bedside table. As the train moves off toward Falkirk, it is tempting to daydream by the window, but make sure you head to the dining car for a lavish afternoon tea of triangle salmon sandwiches, scones with clotted cream, and slabs of sticky Dundee cake. As crystal and china clink beneath the murmur of small talk, now is the time to make friends with your fellow passengers who will be your dining, walking, and drinking pals for the week ahead.

After climbing up Glen Falloch, with waterfalls aplenty, the train continues north to the village of Spean Bridge for the night where you should sleep soundly without the motion of the train to disturb a post-dinner slumber. When you wake, steel yourself for The Full Scottish breakfast, which features eggs of your choice along with crisp back bacon, haggis, black pudding, potato scones, and pork sausages splitting their skins. Vegetarians, do not despair: there is plenty of crushed avocado on homemade bread, creamy Scottish porridge, and compotes with yogurt and fruit.

With no expense spared on rich furnishings and liveried stewards topping up champagne, it is only natural that the train's chef is a culinary whiz. Having trained in Michelin-starred restaurants, Mark Tamburrini is not only adept at creating seasonal menus, but can also prepare them in a six-by-two-meter carriage, sending out steaming plates of Rannoch Moor venison with whorls of turnip fondant and perfectly trailed juniper jus.

During breakfast, the train passes through Fort William with views of Ben Nevis and the famous Glenfinnan Viaduct. From here the route snakes north toward the Arisaig coastline, where passengers can disembark for a bracing walk along the beach. Known as the Silver Sands of Morar, the area is actually a string of beaches with grassy pathways and wind-battered dunes. After working up a good appetite, it is back on board for a hearty lunch followed by an afternoon of exploration around Glenfinnan with yet another afternoon tea in the nineteenth century Inverlochy Castle Hotel.

When you have some downtime, make the most of the onboard lounge and feel free to slink off to the observation car even if no one else is about. It is an ideal spot for sipping a cup of tea and watching the landscape rise and fall around you, the clean Scottish air clearing your lungs. The next day passengers set off for a full day off-board, starting with a ferry ride across to the Isle of Bute to Mount Stuart, which dates back to 1719. The Bute Collection houses astounding artwork by artists including Thomas Gainsborough, Henry Raeburn, and Richard Brakenburgh, along with a first folio by Shakespeare and a book annotated by Robert Burns.

The train now takes a pause in the journey, dropping off passengers in Edinburgh for the day before embarking upon the next leg of the adventure toward the north. Through Fife and Perth, the train runs right along the coast through Arbroath, Montrose, and Aberdeen, arriving in the market town of Keith. Passengers will be whisked higher still to Inverness, the capital of the Highlands, sitting at the mouth of the River Ness. From here you will experience one of the loveliest sections of railroad in the country as the train journeys toward the Kyle of Lochalsh, amid a network of ice-blue lochs and mountains. Over the next few days, expect an excess of everything from windy walks and castles to massages and the heady morning scent of bacon. On the final night, the entertainment is usually a *ceilidh:* these traditional Scottish dances can seem confusing at first, but a whiskey will help you make sense of it all. And then it is off to bed: one last cozy night being rocked to sleep by the motion of the train as it winds its way back to Edinburgh. ◆

*Point of interest:*
*Cairngorms National Park with*
*five of the six highest mountains*
*in the U.K.*

*Make sure to:*
*dress for the occasion. A jacket*
*and tie is expected for informal*
*dinners but formal dining*
*requires black tie or kilts, and*
*cocktail dresses or the equivalent*

Much of the journey is spent away
from the train, walking wild moors,
climbing hills, and exploring the
Scottish countryside.

*On the final night, the entertainment is usually a ceilidh: these traditional Scottish dances can seem confusing at first, but a whiskey will help you make sense of it all.*

Prepare yourself for a week of whiskey, haggis, neeps and tatties, along with Scottish castles, tartan kilts, and dancing.

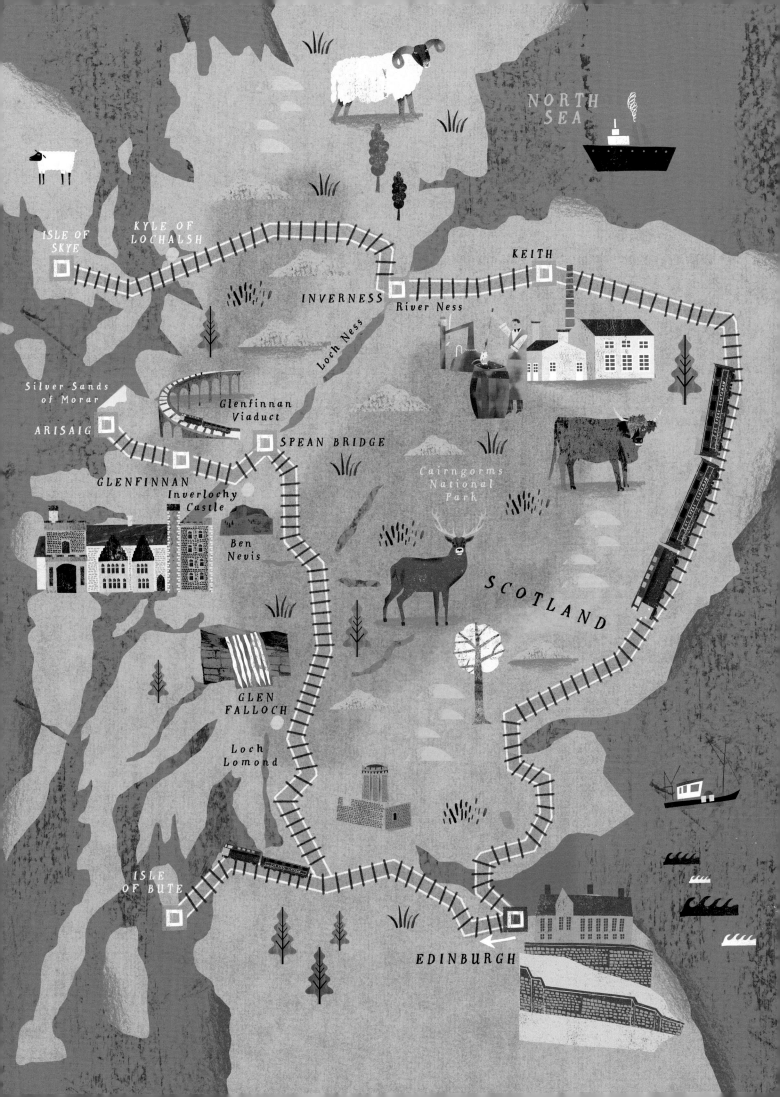

# Venice Simplon-Orient-Express

*It is the most famous train in the world. And for one night only, passengers can dress up, drink up, and reignite the romance of rail travel.*

FROM VENICE, ITALY TO LONDON, U.K.
1 NIGHT

From Agatha Christie and Ian Fleming to Robert Baden-Powell and Mata Hari, the Orient Express has forever captivated authors, spies, dancers, and royalty, featuring as the glamorous backdrop to action movies and advertisements for Chanel No. 5. It is no surprise that this fabulous train regularly ranks number one on lists of the best train journeys in the world.

Arriving at Venezia Santa Lucia station, passengers will be able to spot the blue and gold beauty in a heartbeat. Highly polished and prompting curious stares, the 1920s carriages are an enduring symbol of the romance of train travel. To the envy of Italian commuters watching from afar, you will be relieved of your luggage by a steward, who will transport them to your compartment—and offer a glass of prosecco in return. From then on, you are on holiday and free to inspect the various cars while the gentle sound of *Bésame Mucho* drifts up the corridors from a grand piano.

Despite the pleasing narratives that float about on board, there was never an "original" Orient Express. Launched in 1883, the Orient Express was no more than a regular passenger service incorporating numerous different sets of rolling stock until the golden age of air travel led to its demise. This particular version of the train, known as the Venice Simplon-Orient-Express, was the brainchild of the late James Sherwood, an American businessman who, inspired by British nostalgia for luxury train travel, bought two 1920s carriages and a few marquetry panels at an auction in the 1970s. He then made it his goal to locate as many old cars as he could, eventually finding 23 that he could string together to form a train.

Built from 60 different types of wood in total, these vintage carriages have been lovingly restored to their former glory, down to the last inch of marquetry, and sealed with 15 layers of varnish to give them their mirror-like gleam and squeak.

As the train gathers pace, a gentleman in a tuxedo will knock on your compartment door offering a choice of two sittings for lunch, at which point, it is time to freshen up. Now, with a steady drum of wheels on steel, the train begins to rock through the Dolomites as passengers relax in one of three dining cars, amid the clang of pans coming through the pantry car door. Every time it swings, the smell of warm bread wafts by, before a plate of chicken oysters and foie gras lasagna appears on the snowy white cloth.

To avoid fires on board, the chefs cook without oil and nothing is ever fried, giving the menus an interesting edge. Steady the trembling glasses as the train curves around bends, and take the opportunity to size up your fellow passengers, most of whom will be honeymooning couples, families celebrating birthdays, and hedge-fund managers on a break. Beware that although the set menu is included in your ticket price, anything ordered from the *à la carte* and drinks menu comes with a hefty extra charge.

With the afternoon stretched out ahead, there is nothing sweeter than putting your feet up in the privacy of your compartment with a copy of *Murder on the Orient Express* and a digestif, or taking a cat nap in the sun. Other passengers beeline for the piano car, clinking gin and tonics, clicking cameras, and running fingers along the furniture, tickled at their luxurious surroundings. At night, however, the curtain rises on a truly decadent show. Men in black tie nuzzle in the necks of ladies wearing elbow gloves and flapper headbands, and waiters deftly catch bottles and plates as the train hugs the Austrian Alps. While you dine, your bed will be made up by your steward, your dressing gown laid on the duvet, and you will wake the following morning in Paris to a basket of freshly baked croissants and perfectly brewed coffee—but save space for a brunch of sweet lobster and scrambled eggs.

Owing to logistics, the train can travel only as far as Calais, ending with a fairly grey ride alongside the highway—but after a brief coach trip under the English Channel, a beautiful British Pullman service awaits you on the other side, and covers the final leg from Kent to London Victoria, serving salmon sandwiches and tea before gasping its last breath just after dark. ♦

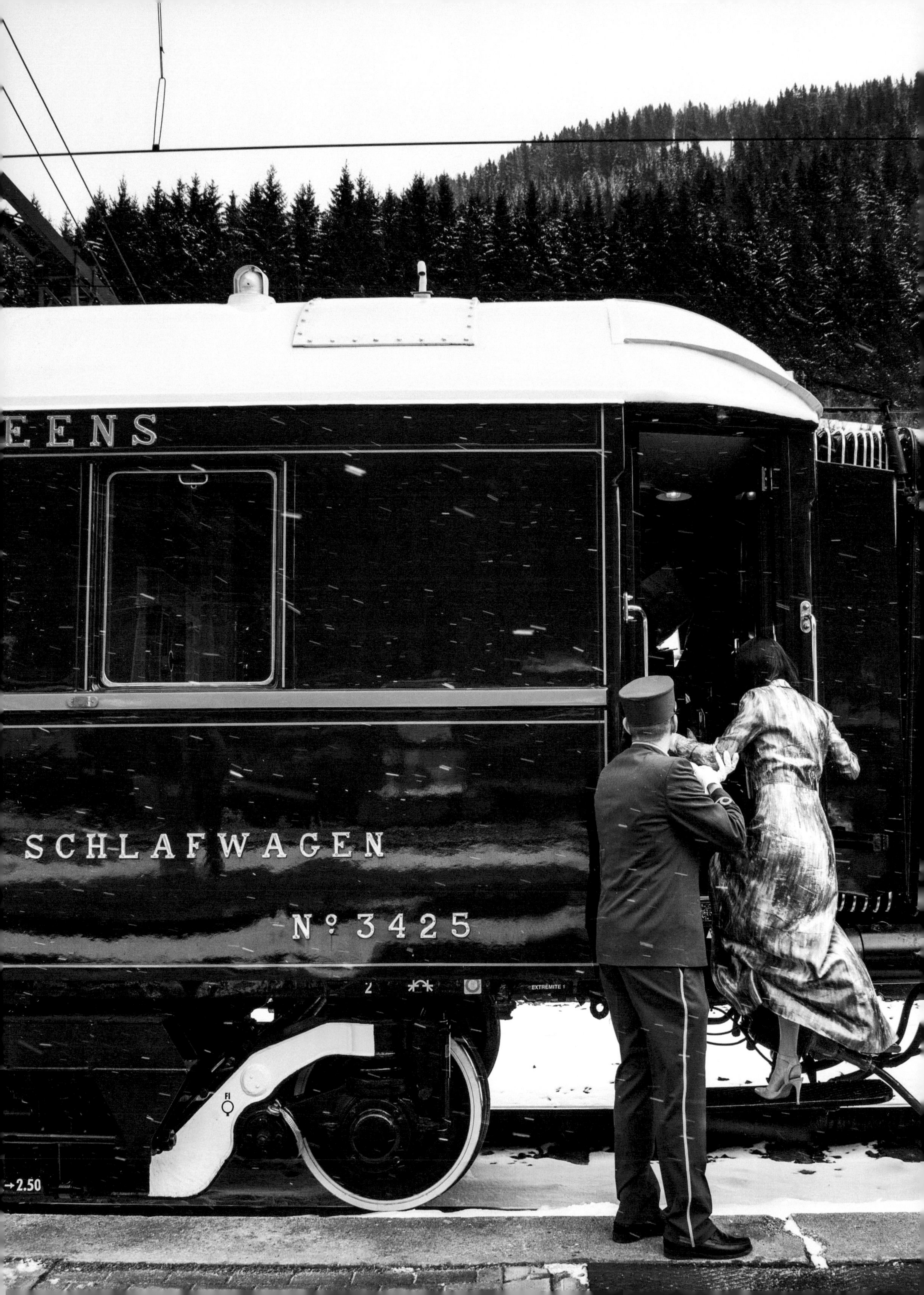
EENS
SCHLAFWAGEN
Nº 3425
2.50

*Point of interest:*
*the unique scenery of the*
*Dolomites*

*Make sure to:*
*dress up to the nines. As the*
*train guide says: "In keeping*
*with the spirit of the occasion,*
*you can never be overdressed*
*on board"*

Traveling in both directions—
from London to Venice and vice
versa—the train that most
passengers prefer is the one that
starts in Venice, as the choppy
waters twinkle past your window.

With the afternoon stretched out ahead, there is nothing sweeter than putting your feet up in the privacy of your compartment with a copy of Murder on the Orient Express *and a digestif.*

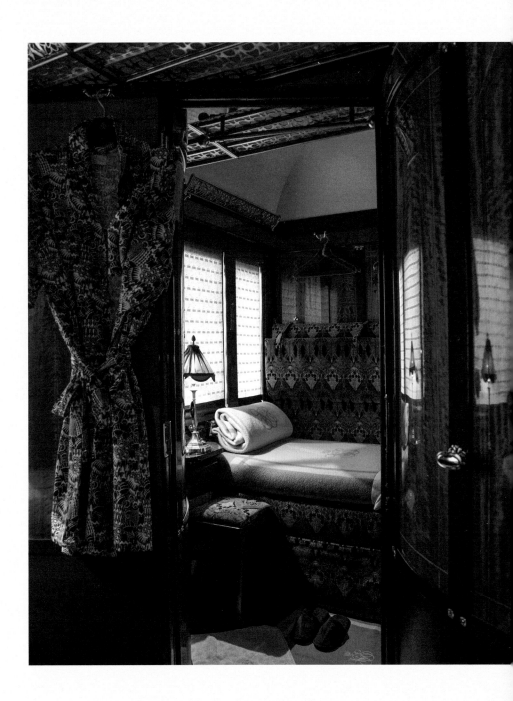

Contrary to popular belief, there was no "original" Orient Express. Launched in 1883, the Orient Express was a regular passenger service incorporating several sets of rolling stock. Its current form is a homage to the romance of rail travel.

# Uncovering the History of the Route

*Whether it is colonial roots, a war-torn past, or a legacy of rescue, the trains we travel always have a story to tell.*

As the world opens up and the search for adventure begins, the need for slow travel is more pressing than ever. It is no longer enough to fly and flop, skimming the surface of a city without investing in its culture, people, and history. And when it comes to railroads, there is often a deep and complex history behind their construction.

It is no secret that European powers rampaged around the world draining countries of their resources. However, colonial defenders will often begin their argument with: "But what about the railways?" Ignoring the fact that many countries developed a railroad system without the devastation of colonization, apologists for empire assume the railroads were a gift. The British Raj built India's network as a fast-track plan to govern more efficiently, facilitate the plunder of loot, and line their pockets at the expense of the local taxpayer who footed the bill (yet was not allowed to travel on board). In Africa, Cecil Rhodes's plan to build the red line from Cairo to Cape Town was an attempt to link all British dominions, and included segregation long before Apartheid.

Trains have often been used as political tools and weapons of war, with both Hitler and Pol Pot exploiting railroads to transport unsuspecting citizens to their deaths; and during the Second World War, Japan used Allied Prisoners of War and civilians to build a railroad in the hope of invading northeast India. Now known as the Death Railway, owing to the number of prisoners who perished during its construction, a segment of track still runs from Bangkok's Thonburi station to Nam Tok. There is a museum at the end of the line to commemorate the loss, with oral testimonies available for visitors to listen to as they walk through the old sleepers that disappear into the jungle.

However, trains have also played the roles of saviors through some of history's greatest tragedies: when America dropped the atomic bomb on Hiroshima, turning the city to a steaming mass of burning bodies and black rain, the trains were up and running almost immediately, with survivors shoving wounded family and friends through the windows and doors in an attempt to flee the nuclear fallout. More widely known is the way in which trains were used to help children escape the Nazis on Kindertransport.

There is a certain poignancy that comes from learning about these stories while riding the very trains on which they took place. While traveling from Hiroshima to Nagasaki, I read the story of Tsutomu Yamaguchi, a Mitsubishi engineer who had survived the first bomb and boarded the train in a desperate attempt to get home to his family in Nagasaki. As I looked out across the same seas that he would have passed, I could feel a sense of desperation, knowing that he had arrived in Nagasaki only to be bombed a second time. Incredibly, he survived both, eventually dying from stomach cancer in 2010, at the age of 93. As a starting point, Christian Wolmar's numerous railroad histories provide excellent accounts of rails through the ages. It is certainly worth picking up a couple to read during your travels. ♦

# The Trans-Mongolian Railway

*Carrying passengers across the largest country in the world and beyond, this godfather of trains offers close encounters, vodka shots, and memories to last a lifetime.*

FROM MOSCOW, RUSSIA TO BEIJING, CHINA
6 NIGHTS

Tell a local Russian that the Trans-Siberian is on your bucket list, and they may laugh in your face. For most Russian people, the train is nothing more than a commuter service, and a dated one at that, carrying soldiers, laborers, lawyers, and large families across remote territory where highways and airports are practically non-existent. Announced by Tsar Alexander III in 1891, construction of the railroad began through forests, marshes, swamps, and frozen lakes, and was finally completed in 1916, connecting Vladivostok in the East with Moscow in the West, an incredible 5,772 miles (9,289 kilometers) away. However, its sister route, the Trans-Mongolian, is the more popular choice for travelers looking for variation in terms of scenery, food, and passengers.

Spanning 4,735 miles (7,621 kilometers), the Trans-Mongolian departs from Moscow's Yaroslavsky station and takes six nights to cross Siberia and Mongolia before worming down into China. Once you have boarded, deposited bags, and found your berth, go for a wander to locate your *provodnik* or *provodnitsa*. Best likened to an attendant or conductor, they are responsible for wake-up calls, locking toilets at stations, and managing the general order in the carriage, so it is worth getting on their good side quite early with a generous tip or two.

Unless you have booked onto the plush Rossiya service with its soft berths and sliding doors, the domestic train will already reek of dried omul, long and thin as though ironed into strips. This yellowing fish is a staple in the makeshift pantries set up by passengers, along with loaves of bread, cartons of juice, and rounds of cheese wrapped in wet cloth. There is a samovar in each carriage with constant boiling water, so make sure to pack enough instant noodles, soups, and sachets of coffee, along with fruit and dried snacks to keep you going for the six-day journey.

There is no need to panic if you are under-stocked, though. Follow the exhausting sound of Euro-trance music to the dining car, where you will find a couple of chefs wearing shorts under aprons, and invariably a waitress with gold teeth. Menus are delightfully old with frayed laminate edges, but the food is perfectly decent if you are happy with fried pork *escalopes* and fries, enthusiastically draped with dill. There is also a trolley stacked with every snack from Pringles and Kit-Kats to instant mash and a fridge full of beer.

By now the train will be sailing through the bleakness of Moscow's suburbs: tower blocks, graffiti-covered bridges, and ugliness abound, with the odd golden dome of an Orthodox church gleaming through the grey—so settle in for the long ride. While it is possible to book one ticket all the way through to Beijing, it is more usual to break up the journey in Irkutsk to explore the magical Lake Baikal by steam train, then again in Ulaanbaatar, from where you can travel out onto the Mongolian steppe to ride or stay with nomads. However, if you want to do this, it is important to book each leg in advance.

*By now the train will be sailing through the bleakness of Moscow's suburbs: tower blocks, graffiti-covered bridges, and ugliness abound, with the odd golden dome of an Orthodox church gleaming through the grey—so settle in for the long ride.*

For the brave souls facing six continuous nights, the journey may become a blur of leafless birch trees flitting by the window, futile attempts to read *War and Peace*, playing cards—and drinking with companions. It is not unusual to find lone travelers eating home-packed cottage cheese blinis with a four-pack of Stella Artois on the side, which they will no doubt want to share (the blinis, not the beer). And this is where the spirit of the journey lies.

Soldiers down vodka shots, question your allegiance to President Putin, and scroll through photos on your phone before giving a beery thumbs-up in approval. Even if languages are not common, there is always a mutual understanding between →

→ each party, and as the miles accumulate, the shared experience of pleasures and pains is spurred by the natural symbiosis unique to train travel.

Even though there are around 80 stops along the route, most last for no longer than a few minutes, but when there is a good hour's stop approaching the *provodnik* will let you know so that you can get your shoes on, find some cash, and head out onto the platform to stock up on baskets of tiny wild strawberries and roast chicken wrapped in cling film—or, if you're feeling brave, strips of dried omul that are usually speared through the eye like a bunch of keys and touted around by ladies in neon Lycra.

*But when all is quiet at night, it is a good time to slip down from your berth and stand in the corridor alone watching Siberia's red skies bleed into silver lakes, and mists embracing forests. In that quiet of night while everyone sleeps, a kind of magic lights up the darkness.*

Much like a mobile camping trip, this journey allows you to reap what you sow, so make friends, offer drinks around, and be open to curious conversation. But when all is quiet at night, it is a good time to slip down from your berth and stand in the corridor alone watching Siberia's red skies bleed into silver lakes, and mists embracing forests. In that quiet of night while everyone sleeps, a kind of magic lights up the darkness. Smoke winds out of skinny, naked woods, and voices drift in from apparently empty platforms. This is a part of the world that most travelers never get to see, this hinge in the earth where the West meets the East in a strange kind of no-man's-land, the train shining a light into its darkest corners.

As the train leaves Siberia and enters Mongolia, the ground warms up to a thirsty, rust-red terrain. Round nomadic yurts appear, their funnels piping smoke into the skies, and wild horses nibble tufts of yellowing grass. Passengers look different here, too: where once they were blond with blue eyes,

then blond with dark eyes, they are now dark-haired with dark eyes, a gradation of features evolving with the landscape. Over the previous few days, the train has witnessed the skies close in, the seas pull apart, and the land unlock. Mountains have emerged then flattened, and as the train thunders toward China's capital city, billboards appear, wires sag low, and buildings shuffle toward the tracks, filling passengers with an undeniable sense of purpose and place. Finally, slowing into the station, the train creaks and comes to a halt. Through the roar of the crowd, the rolling of cases, and muffled announcements, step onto the platform and allow Beijing to sweep you into its embrace. ◆

Lake Baikal is the deepest, oldest, and largest freshwater lake in the world. Formed in the middle of a giant crack in the Earth's crust—the Baikal rift—the lake was dubbed the "Galápagos of Russia" by UNESCO, owing to the unique species of flora and fauna.

*Point of interest:*
the Chinese border crossing at
Erlian where the train is jacked
up and the chassis changed
with passengers still on board

*Make sure to:*
pack plenty of food and drink
for the long journey

A lack of roads through Russia means that local people are condemned to using the Trans-Mongolian as their only means of transport to visit family or travel for work: one person's bucket-list adventure is another's nightmare commute.

BELARUS

UKRAINE

MOSCOW

Ural Mountains

TRANS-SIBERIAN RAILWAY

Caspian Sea

AZER-
BAIJAN

KAZAKHSTAN

UZBEKISTAN

TURKMENISTAN

IRAN

KYRGYZSTAN

# The Golden Eagle

*Traversing the old Silk Road from Kazakhstan to Uzbekistan and Turkmenistan to Russia, this luxury train offers an energetic tour of Central Asia.*

FROM ALMATY, KAZAKHSTAN TO MOSCOW, RUSSIA
12 DAYS

An unfair reputation precedes Kazakhstan, thanks to a certain British comedian; however, its capital city, Almaty, is far from a rural outpost, with a KFC, a Costa coffee shop, and the highest ice-skating rink in the world. With tree-lined boulevards, and woods concealing beautiful multicolored cathedrals tipped with gold, Almaty is a cultural melting pot and a fascinating place to start your journey on the Golden Eagle. You will be taken to the edge of the city, where a cable car ride gives an eye-level view of the surrounding Tian Shan mountains, their wizened old heads greyed with ice. Then it is back on board for the overnight journey to Tashkent. With three levels of service, the train offers a range of comfort from small double beds with en suite facilities in silver class, to power showers and underfloor heating in gold class, right up to imperial suites with their libraries and lounge areas. Waking in the cosmopolitan Uzbek capital, passengers spend the day walking around what remains of the old town before journeying on to Samarkand and Bukhara—havens of ancient Islamic architecture, food, and culture. With time to yourself, follow the sweet smell of dried fruit around the cities' backstreets, taste the skewers of grilled meat and flavored tea, and do not forget to shop. Back on board the Golden Eagle, passengers settle in for dinner and an evening of desert scenery before arriving in Turkmenistan to the sun-kissed sight of fountains and golden domes. It is a packed itinerary that then takes passengers on to Khiva, Volgograd, and Moscow, but in between strolling through bazaars, and visiting mosques and museums, there is plenty of time to unwind on board. ◆

Built in 1712, the beautiful Bolo Hauz Mosque in Bukhara is one of the few preserved in Uzbekistan's capital. Supported by 20 wooden pillars, the mosque is instantly recognizable in the Registan district.

Take a whirlwind tour through the heart of Central Asia, while sipping tea and watching deserts sweep past the window from the warmth and comfort of a luxury cabin.

*Point of interest:*
*the burning gas crater*
*at Darvaza*

*Make sure to:*
*dress appropriately when*
*visiting mosques and other*
*places of worship*

# Qinghai-Tibet Railway

*In spite of its turbulent history, Tibet remains one of the few naturally beautiful regions in the world, much of which is visible from this train.*

FROM XINING, CHINA TO LHASA, TIBET AUTONOMOUS REGION
21 HOURS

Picture electric blue skies, blazing yellow sands, and lakes shimmering like molten metal—and you just might come close to conjuring the magnificence of the Qinghai-Tibet Plateau. The highest and largest plateau in the world, it is bound by the Kunlun Mountains to the northeast, and the Himalayas to the southwest, with a high-speed train running in between.

As you might imagine, this was not ideal terrain on which to build a railroad. Not only does it hold the record for both the world's highest track and highest station at Tanggula, it also speeds through earthquake zones along 300 miles (483 kilometers) of track built on permafrost that can melt at the slightest increase in temperature—a problem that engineers solved by circulating liquid nitrogen below the rail bed in an attempt to keep it frozen year-round.

It is important to bear in mind, though, that despite being a technical marvel, the railroad has posed an ecological threat to natural reserves and endangered species such as snow leopards. Its arrival in 2006 was greeted with mixed emotions: most Tibetans were filled with dismay, seeing the railroad as little more than another means by which Han Chinese settlers could continue to colonize their homeland, while others living close to the proposed stations were excited by the prospect of business and employment for their towns.

Traveling to Tibet can certainly conjure up complicated feelings of unease in the face of the autonomous region's bloody history, which continues into the present. In the 1950s, Chinese military forces seized and occupied Tibet, killing and torturing monks, before destroying the majority of Buddhist monasteries during the Cultural Revolution, causing the Dalai Lama to flee to India where he remains in exile. Pleading to the world in vain, the kingdom was absorbed into China, and restrictions are currently placed upon its ethnic people, who are forbidden from traveling in and out, or showing allegiance to the Dalai Lama—whether through speech, praying, or keeping images of him in their homes.

However, the Dalai Lama has himself encouraged travelers to visit Tibet and to describe their experiences upon their return. Foreigners also offer a vital communication link for Tibetans who have no other contact with the outside world.

Most tourists prefer to fly into the capital of Lhasa, rather than endure the 21-hour train journey, but traveling by train reveals the soul of the land in a way that can never be felt while peering down from a grubby plane window. It also allows travelers to stagger the ascent so that the onset of altitude sickness is minimized. Not everyone will suffer from the usual symptoms of headaches and nausea, but it is important nevertheless to stay well hydrated and drink more than you usually would, avoiding alcohol.

*The Qinghai-Tibet Plateau is the highest and largest in the world and is bound by the Kunlun Mountains to the northeast, and the Himalayas to the southwest, with a high-speed train running in between.*

Departing from Xining, a cultural city of temples, mosques, and parks, the comfortable sleeper service travels through darkness—an unavoidable frustration that means passengers miss views of the magical Qinghai Lake that appears shortly after the evening departure. No matter in which direction you travel, the length of the journey means that some part of it will have to take place overnight.

The following morning you will wake in pitch darkness to the hiss of enriched oxygen being pumped into your compartment through tiny gold nozzles. Ascending to a peak of 16,640 feet (5,072 meters) above sea level, the train is fitted with a supply to help travelers adjust to the altitude. Oxygen is supposed to be odorless, but the cold stream often reeks of old cigarettes. There are clear signs in the vestibules—both in English and Chinese—forbidding passengers from smoking between Golmud and Lhasa, but this →

→ does little to deter the more stubborn ones, who often hide in the toilets and light up.

Shuffle up to the window and pull up the blackout blind to a blaze of light that will make you recoil. Once your eyes have adjusted, you will see miles and miles of golden plateau with gently sloping hills forming a perfect ridge against the skies. Nowhere else in the world looks like this, as though the Earth has been filtered into technicolor: mountains of white ice dazzle in the sunshine, green waters appear radioactive, and strips of prayer flags dance in the wind like jubilant kite tails.

Over the next few hours, it is easy to spot shabby-looking yaks standing around like balls of tumbleweed, red bells slung around their necks. The sources of rivers slide down the ice-blue Kunlun Mountains, and on the approach to Lhasa, they shrink into chocolate brown hills with sugarcoated tops.

*When you disembark from the train you will feel a sharpness in your lungs like never before: the taste of the cleanest, purest air. Eyes will water in the wind, cheeks will sting in the sun.*

Given the restrictions on Tibetans' travel, it is only in the final few stops that passengers will notice locals boarding the train. With wind-burnt complexions and cheeks as burnished as apples, they are easy to spot with ribbons plaited into their hair, and baskets and babies on their backs.

Almost everyone has an idea of what Tibet looks like, perhaps with monasteries, monks in red robes, and cloudless, perfect skies. However, the reality can be a shock: on the approach to the capital, the land levels out and flat-roofed houses begin to huddle toward the track. Built from grey brick and blue tiles, each has a front yard planted with a bright red Chinese flag. A Mitsubishi manufacturer and a Buick garage will sail by the window along with an avenue lined with Chinese flags, indicating that the city is drawing in.

Here, passengers might sense that Tibet is no longer the Shangri-La of dreams: the streets are filled with Porsche Cayennes, Coca-Cola machines, and monks on their iPhones strolling by in Nike trainers—signs that we live in a global world. Pulling into a space-age hangar of a station, the train is subject to searches, and foreign tourists will have bags scanned with a disconcerting level of severity. Chinese guards stand firm at police gates and checkpoints, and you can expect to see much of the same around the city, at the entrances to every temple and monastery, and even at the beautiful Potala Palace, the Dalai Lama's former home. However, it is important to maintain an open mind and to show a willingness to listen and watch closely during the time you spend in Tibet.

When you disembark from the train, you will feel a sharpness in your lungs like never before: the taste of the cleanest, purest air. Eyes will water in the wind, cheeks will sting in the sun. As you travel around the remaining monasteries and gardens, try to stop by Tibetan-owned restaurants and cafes, and shop in Tibetan-owned boutiques. Above all, be mindful that it is a privilege to witness a culture that is just hanging on by a thread. ◆

Through the final hours of the journey, the weather is often changeable: As the train descends into valleys, clouds move in, obscuring the tops of suede-soft mountains, greyed with ice and snow.

*Point of interest:*
*the Tanggula Pass—the highest*
*railroad point in the world*

*Make sure to:*
*acclimatize to the altitude in*
*Xining if you can*

On the approach to Lhasa, icy
mountains shrink down into softer,
chocolate-brown hills, their heads
sugarcoated with snow.

*Shuffle up to the window and pull up the blackout blind to a blaze of light that will make you recoil. Once your eyes have adjusted, you will see miles and miles of golden plateau with gently sloping hills forming a perfect ridge against the skies.*

The dining car is the hub of the action, but do not worry if your service does not have one. A regular trolley service passes up the aisles selling yogurts, fruit, noodles, and drinks.

CHINA

KUNLUN MOUNTAINS

TIBET

QINGHAI LAKE

XINING

GOLMUD

TANGGULA MOUNTAINS

TANGGULA

NAGCHU

LHASA

HIMALAYAS

NEPAL

BHUTAN

BANGLADESH

INDIA

MYANMAR

# Beijing to Shanghai

*Forget long queues, check-ins, and security. The fastest, most efficient, and punctual way to travel between China's megacities is on the bullet train.*

FROM BEIJING TO SHANGHAI, CHINA
4 HOURS 18 MINUTES

Arriving into the airy atrium of Beijing South Railway Station—one of the largest train stations in Asia—you feel like you are in the center of a glass shopping mall or a sports stadium. Like much of the capital's modern infrastructure, the station was one of a number of projects whizzed through in time for the 2008 Olympic Games. It took 4,000 workers just two-and-a-half years to complete, replacing Yongdingmen station, a piece of architectural beauty that had dated back to 1897. It was the first—and the prototype—of China's high-speed stations, and if you stand on the top-floor balcony it is quite a sight to witness the bullet trains lined up and ready to shoot off. Although there is a trolley service on board the Beijing to Shanghai line, serving iced coffee and movie-theater-style tubs of ice cream, there is no traditional dining car for a leisurely meal, so it is worth picking up something to keep you going from one of the station's many fast-food outlets.

Taking the train in China used to mean choosing between a hard- or soft-sleeper berth, filling a flask of tea, and hanging out in the heat of the dining car on a long and noisy ride. Joyful with the clamor of passengers clearing throats, watching soaps on glittery iPhones, and shelling peanuts onto the floor, Chinese trains can often feel like a microcosm of a city on the move. Outside the carriage, the country's mountains, orchards, and grey seas pass by at a moderate pace, slowly enough for you to lean out of a window and breathe it in. But that is all changing fast.

Taking after neighboring Japan, China launched its first newly built high-speed line in 2003 with a 251-mile (405-kilometer) route between Qinhuangdao and Shenyang, for trains running up to 155 mph (250 km/h). Boldly ambitious plans for a high-speed network made the rest of the world watch with bemusement, but in as little as 18 years, China has completed construction of more than 23,500 miles (37,900 kilometers) of high-speed track, with trains running at a maximum speed of 220 mph (350 km/h).

While it is still perfectly possible, and enormously fun, to board a 19-hour sleeper service, it is equally intriguing to step inside the high-speed G train and make the same journey in as little as four hours.

The *Gaotie* high-speed train, which covers 819 miles (1,318 kilometers) between Beijing and Shanghai, is the preferred choice of business travelers and the wealthy middle class who have no time or patience for shambling, delayed sleeper trains. However, for all the upsides, there are downsides too: there is a tangible absence of the romance of rail travel here, with nothing but the warm fug of KFC filling the aisles, and the occasional musical announcement. Most passengers ignore one another, shoving in earphones, reclining their flatbeds in business class, or reading newspapers— so do not expect much conversation. Like Japan's Shinkansen, the G trains offer no more than a means to get from one destination to the other—but there is one phenomenon that will hold your attention.

Every half hour or so it is typical to see concrete clusters of empty tower blocks covered with tarps and cranes. The skeleton structures look like Lego cities emerging from the middle of nowhere. Dubbed China's "ghost cities," these hubs first emerged in Shenzhen in 1978, but began to multiply at an alarming rate all over the country after a government push to boost GDP and develop infrastructure in China's more remote areas. Although the trains are traveling at extraordinary speeds and most of what you will see will be blurred, if you look hard enough you can sometimes make out sports stadiums and shopping malls alongside the towers, all of which were designed to attract rural communities or citizens from overflowing megacities in search of lower rents and a better quality of life.

As the train approaches Shanghai Hongqiao station, you will see the city's skyscrapers and neon lights flashing in the distance. Passengers will begin to redo their hair, pull on jackets, and rummage around for lost shoes, and you will feel a surge of excitement that you are about to experience one of the most energetic cities in the world. ◆

*Points of interest:*
*keep an eye out for the*
*clusters of ghost cities that*
*pop up along the way*

*Make sure to:*
*have a wander down the*
*carriages to check out*
*the different classes*

Business-class passengers can expect
a premium experience to rival that
of air travel. Tickets include priority
boarding, free beverages and meals,
and red leather seats that convert into
flatbeds, with a reading light and
buzzer to call an attendant.

*As the train approaches Shanghai Hongqiao station, you will see the city's skyscrapers and neon lights flashing in the distance. And you will feel a surge of excitement that you are about to experience one of the most energetic cities in the world.*

The Great Wall of China is easily accessible by train from Beijing. Passengers disembark at Badaling and can walk sections of the wall which, oddly enough, have been rebuilt to resemble a crumbling style.

BEIJING

TIANJIN

JINAN

YELLOW RIVER

CHINA

NANJING

SUZHOU

SHANGHAI

YANGTZE RIVER

# Shanghai Maglev

*In the face of advancing technology, trains are sleeker, safer, and faster than ever—as this eight-minute zip across the city will prove.*

FROM PUDONG INTERNATIONAL AIRPORT
TO LONGYANG ROAD, SHANGHAI, CHINA
8 MINUTES

Bring out your inner child with a ride on one of the fastest trains in the world. With a maximum speed of 267 mph (430 km/h), the Shanghai Maglev takes only eight minutes to cover the 19 miles (31 kilometers) between the Shanghai Pudong International Airport and Longyang Road stations. Largely intended to transport airport arrivals into the Chinese megacity, the train is often frequented at the weekends by young families and thrill-seeking adults entertaining themselves with selfie sticks and a round trip. Launched at the end of 2002, Shanghai's system was then the only commercial maglev in operation in the world. A hybrid of "magnetic levitation," the high-speed train has no wheels. Instead, a magnetized coil called a guideway runs along the track, repelling large magnets fixed to the underside of the train. This causes the train to levitate above the guideway, and then a series of magnetic fields pull and push it along. Given that the maglev is effectively floating on a cushion of air, there is no friction, so the movement resembles that of an airplane as you strap in and brace against the surge. Be sure to sit by the window so you can watch apartment blocks, freeways, and parks shoot by so fast you can barely fix your eyes on anything. Overhead, a digital speedometer tells you when the train has reached its peak speed before it arrives into the roar of the city. ♦

104

Do not be embarrassed to buy a round-trip ticket for the sheer joy of riding the train. You will be in the company of other tourists and young families enjoying the roller-coaster speeds.

# North Korea by Train

*Reputation precedes the so-called hermit kingdom, but 10 days on a chartered train around the country offers an invaluable peek behind the curtain.*

FROM PYONGYANG TO PYONGYANG, NORTH KOREA
10 DAYS

It may come as a surprise to know that tourists have been allowed to visit North Korea since 1953, after an armistice ended the Korean War. However, until 1988, tourism was restricted to visitors from fellow communist countries, or "friendly" countries of the Non-Aligned Movement, which included Indonesia, India, Egypt, Yugoslavia, and Ghana among a handful of developing nations that refused to identify with the ideologies of the Western and Eastern blocs.

Although independent travel is impossible, privately run companies offer guided tours into the country from Beijing, one of which is a 10-day train tour. Much like a cruise on wheels, groups spend the day on board, watching the scenery go by, eating freshly cooked lunches, and chatting to the guides, before disembarking to spend the night in hotels or visit sites of interest.

The decision to travel to North Korea is not one to be taken lightly, and careful consideration should be given as to whether you are willing to observe regulations with regards to photography, engaging in political discourse with guides, and bowing to statues of the leaders. Even though the country's current leader is Kim Jong Un, North Korea is considered a necrocracy—meaning that it is still ruled by the dead. Statues of both the founding father, Kim Il Sung, and his son, Kim Jong Il, are commonplace in every city, and visitors are given a bunch of flowers to place at their feet and a moment to bow. When taking photographs of the statues you must include their entire body, rather than cropping them. All of this may seem extreme, but doing otherwise could put your tour guides at risk of punishment.

Once you decide to visit, the process is straightforward, and your tour company will organize visas, accommodation, and travel from Beijing to North Korea and back. Interaction and communication between foreign tourists and citizens is heavily restricted, so travelers are not allowed on local trains. Instead, you will find yourself on board a much smarter-looking chartered train comprising old Swiss carriages with pull-down windows, perfect for leaning out and inhaling the smell of fields between stops.

Starting in the capital city of Pyongyang, the route covers the cities of Hyangsan, Wonsan, Hamhung, and the port city of Chongjin, giving passengers a rare opportunity to see beyond the confines of Pyongyang where most foreign visits begin and end. If you are used to the fizz and energy of Asian cities, it can feel unnerving to arrive in Pyongyang where there is an absence of both. Streets are tank-wide but free from honking, hawkers, traffic, fumes, chatter, and color. Billboards blaze propagandist messages of pride and glory: strong-jawed young men raising scythes and fists with missiles soaring in the background. Apartment blocks are no more than four-stories high with pots of red flowers on the balconies.

*Much like a cruise on wheels, groups spend the day on board, watching the scenery go by, eating freshly cooked lunches, and chatting to the guides, before disembarking to spend the night in hotels or visit sites of interest.*

Years of gazing at cities by night will have wired in you an expectation of flashing neon, the ruby necklace of brake lights from crawling traffic, and street lights—none of which you will see from your hotel window. Only the red flame of the Juche Tower stays aglow, but the rest of Pyongyang melts into the shadows. A spattering of light reveals the odd high rise, but the city looks as though it has been unplugged.

On the first morning of the tour, passengers are transferred by coach to Pyongyang station just as the clock marks the hour, and a wailing tune crackles from loudspeakers like the soundtrack to a sci-fi movie. Above, the two smiling faces of Kim Il Sung and Kim Jong Il loom from the façade— a constant sight around the country. With nothing but the squeak of your own footsteps echoing in your ears, you will enter a station that resembles →

→ a concrete airport hangar: no ticket machines, no passengers, no trains, no whistles, no announcements. Just your group—and one train waiting on a far platform.

This is where the journey really begins, as the train winds out of the city and is soon flanked by fields of bundled corn along which cyclists pedal in the heat. Oxen bow and snort, drawing wooden carts piled with people—don't be tempted to take photographs without their consent. A country's people are the prism through which any understanding is formed; conversations confirm or dispel myths, and anecdotes create an impression, but the void here is a huge one, and being in North Korea can often feel like watching a film with the sound turned off.

From your guides, you will learn about the Kim dynasty, albeit through a highly filtered narrative. Although frustrating, it is polite to accept their version, as an interrogation from a passenger could get them into trouble with their colleagues. Visitors can spend a lot of time muttering to one another in bemusement and wondering how the story of the two benevolent father figures is so widely accepted by citizens. However, defectors to South Korea have begun to describe how fewer people buy into the state propaganda these days, and they are growing more aware and more trusting of foreign media that finds its way into the country on USB sticks and DVDs. Cities on the borders of China and South Korea are often able to pick up foreign TV and radio signals, allowing North Koreans to tune into a different reality.

After the train arrives in each city, you will board a coach and be driven around sights that could include a fertilizer factory, a kindergarten with performing toddlers, a department store with no customers inside—and the mausoleum that houses both of the late leaders in glass cases, which is a surreal experience. In between, it is impossible not to bond with your group through the shared experience, which can take its toll after a few days. You will develop some lifelong friendships by the end—after all, it is not your average person who chooses to visit North Korea for fun.

Traveling around the country by train offers visitors less constrained images of North Korean life, as here you are at least given the chance to observe village life, watch children play games in the street, and receive the reluctant smiles of passers-by who might never have seen a fancy train with foreign faces poking out of the windows. However, the narrative is never as linear as it seems. Politically favored families are granted the privilege of living in Pyongyang, whereas those lower down the scale must live elsewhere and are denied papers that allow them to move between cities. And, like most places in the world, the privileged also receive access to better education and infrastructure—which includes railroad lines. So even though the towns you travel through might appear prosperous, the houses sturdy, and the people healthy, these areas might not reflect the full picture.

*From your guides, you will learn about the Kim dynasty, albeit through a highly filtered narrative. Although frustrating, it is polite to accept their version, as an interrogation from a passenger could get them into trouble with their colleagues.*

On the final leg from Wonsan back to Pyongyang there is a tangible air of sadness that after 10 days, this is your last journey as a "family." From the train, the maple trees seem aflame with fall golds and reds, the river bubbles through the canyon, and the sun darts overhead. Free from the pollution of factories and cars, the air will fill your lungs with freshness, and twinned with an unusually blue sky, it's a joy to hang from the windows. But you will never forget where you are: just around the corner, there is always a looming mural of the Kims, waving and smiling at you. ◆

*Points of interest:*
*the mausoleums housing*
*the embalmed bodies of the*
*two leaders*

*Make sure to:*
*read* Nothing to Envy
*by Barbara Demick,*
*an unrivaled account*
*of life in North Korea*
*from six defectors*
*before the journey*

Traveling to North Korea can
throw up all kinds of questions
about ethical travel, but the
regime's citizens are not to
blame for their leaders' actions.
Already suffering by being cut
off from the rest of the world,
they can only benefit from
increased human interaction.

*Traveling around the country by train offers visitors less constrained images of North Korean life, as here you are at least given the chance to observe village life, watch children play games in the street, and receive the reluctant smiles of passers-by.*

Determined to showcase the best of what the country has to offer, the tour company lays on spreads at every meal which usually include stewed meats, fried eggs, steamed rice, and plenty of spicy kimchi.

CHINA

CHONGJIN

Pujon
Highlands

HYANGSAN

HAMHUNG

SEA OF
JAPAN

WONSAN

PYONGYANG

NORTH
KOREA

# Seven Stars in Kyushu

*Over four days and three nights, this luxury service showcases the cuisine, craftsmanship, and natural beauty of Japan's southernmost main island.*

FROM HAKATA TO HAKATA, JAPAN
4 DAYS, 3 NIGHTS

When you imagine Japanese trains, you probably picture Shinkansen, the bottle-nosed bullet trains that zip around the country in record time. However, Japan's railways encompass much more than pioneering technology, from restaurants on wheels to themed trains that can be chartered for special occasions. Then, of course, there are the luxury services, which the Japanese do with aplomb. The southernmost of Japan's four main islands, Kyushu is home to a fabulous train, so sought after by both foreign and Japanese tourists that hopeful travelers must fill in an application form six months in advance. A hat-tip to the island's seven prefectures, the Seven Stars in Kyushu is the ultimate in opulence: all 14 compartments are suites decorated with artisanal craftsmanship. The interior walls showcase *kumiko,* a traditional method of carpentry by which small, thin pieces of wood are fit together by hand; and the dining car's Arita ware porcelain comes from the 15th generation, family-run Kakiemon kiln in Arita. Completely decked out in wood, and lit by warm lighting, the train feels cozy rather than terrifyingly fancy, with picture frames around the windows and constantly changing countryside flitting past. Mood lighting, soft piano music, and gloved staff on standby can make you feel like you are part of a well-rehearsed performance—but that is all part of the fun. Over four days and three nights, you will be served by various chefs preparing fresh sashimi and dishes steamed with hot spring vapor, but there will also be several opportunities to disembark and dine in backstreet restaurants, stay overnight in a *ryokan* (a traditional Japanese inn), and visit the historic samurai city of Izumi, before returning full circle to Hakata. ♦

From the floors to the ceilings, the Seven Stars in Kyushu is completely decked out in wood, giving it a warm and welcoming atmosphere enhanced by soft lighting and plush interiors.

*Point of interest:*
*the view of Mount Yufu*
*while soaking in the Yufuin*
*Onsen (hot spring) in Oita*

*Make sure to:*
*dress up to the nines*
*for dinner services*
*with renowned chefs*

Renowned chefs rotate
throughout the journey,
preparing traditional
dishes using regional,
seasonal ingredients.

*A hat-tip to the island's seven prefectures, the Seven Stars in Kyushu is the ultimate in opulence: all 14 compartments are suites decorated with artisanal craftsmanship. The interior walls showcase kumiko, a traditional method of carpentry by which small, thin pieces of wood are fit together by hand.*

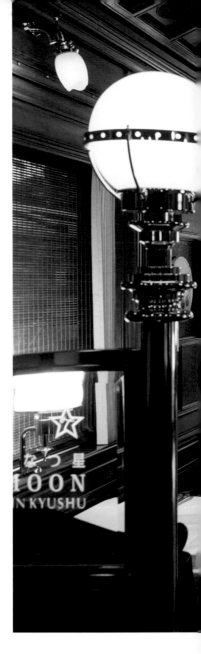

During the day, passengers are welcome to wind down in the quiet of the Blue Moon lounge car, and at night sip a few drinks and mingle with fellow guests to the sound of live music in the background.

# Eastern & Oriental Express

*Harking back to a lost age of luxury travel, Belmond's Southeast Asian service combines the best of the city and the countryside.*

FROM KUALA LUMPUR, MALAYSIA
TO BANGKOK, THAILAND
2 DAYS, 2 NIGHTS

When visiting big Asian cities, it is often easy to forget that just beyond the perimeters lie villages, jungles, and forests—all of which offer an escape from the cities' clamor. Combining the best of both worlds, this two-night journey begins in the sprawl of Kuala Lumpur, then carries passengers overnight into the fresh, green Malaysian countryside, where bent-backed palms line the tracks and drenched paddy fields twinkle in the sun. With 24-hour steward service, slippers left by your bed, and four-course dinners, this is the most decadent way to explore Malaysia and Southern Thailand.

On the first morning, after a breakfast of technicolor local fruit, eggs, and thick, sweet coffee, passengers disembark in the royal town of Kuala Kangsar. From here it is a short coach ride to Labu Kubong, a self-sustaining village in Perak state where residents catch fish with their bare hands, run homestays, and make their own honey. If you are feeling fit, you can go on a hill-trek which peaks with panoramic views of the patchwork quilt of paddies and palms. Then it is back to the train, where you can wash off the day in your private shower, spruce up, and work your way toward the piano bar for a cocktail, before a dinner of plump pan-fried scallops and Nyonya curry washed down with plenty of crisp champagne. The final morning is spent in Kanchanaburi, where thousands of prisoners of war perished during the Second World War while being put to work by the Japanese to build a railroad to Burma. Make sure you visit the Chong Kai War Cemetery and wander the Kwai Yai riverside before departing to Bangkok, where your journey comes to an end. ♦

*Point of interest:*
*Kanchanaburi with the*
*Death Railway Museum*

*Make sure to:*
*dress in loose cotton*
*clothing to stay*
*comfortable during*
*excursions*

The train curls around the Tham Krasae Bridge in Kanchanaburi. Also known as the Wampo Viaduct, this section of the railway was built on wooden trestles by Japan's Allied Prisoners of War.

If you are feeling fit, you
can go on a hill-trek which
peaks with panoramic
views of the patchwork
quilt of paddies and palms.

Over two nights, passengers will travel through the bustle and noise of Kuala Lumpur into the fresh, green countryside, where bent-backed palms line the tracks and waterlogged paddies sparkle in the sun.

# The Death Railway

*With a dark and harrowing history, this beautiful railroad intended to connect Thailand with Burma makes for a somber and memorable journey.*

FROM BANGKOK TO NAM TOK, THAILAND
4.5 HOURS

Pacing the platform at Bangkok's Thonburi station, a growing number of families, backpackers, and smartly dressed retirees sigh and look up at the clock, glancing occasionally down the track. More than half an hour passes before a distant clatter rouses the crowd and the train rolls into view. Gathering bags, water bottles, and various children, passengers clamber onto the train, which creaks beneath the weight of travelers sliding up the benches and yanking open the windows for air. With a jolt, and to a short round of applause, the train moves off and canters through the city, its horn screaming all the way to alert stray cyclists and walkers who might not see it traveling through tall grass.

*Made up of a rattling set of old carriages grouted together with rust, the train rolls into Thonburi station a little before 8:00 a.m.—much to the delight of nervous-looking passengers who can never be too sure that trains will run until they see them arrive.*

A lovely element of Thai trains is the unbridled joy from the passengers, who you could be forgiven for thinking have never ridden on a train before. They kneel on seats, wave at villagers, and let out yelps of glee. As the initial excitement levels out and passengers turn to phones and taking selfies, hawkers call up the carriages carrying colored plastic tubs of treats. Heaving them up to shoulder height, they pad through in flip-flops and baggy shirts, squatting down to show parcels of steamed rice wrapped in cellophane, sticky chicken, freshly grilled satay, and fruit. They forage in buckets of ice, producing cans of coffee and Coke, tucking notes into breast pockets before sliding off the train at the next station. So far, this journey appears to be a typical one, on some of Thailand's loveliest stretches of track, but the reality is that the railway has a marked and harrowing history.

In April 1943, 7,000 Allied Prisoners of War captured by the Japanese were transported in successive trains from Changi prison in Singapore to Ban Pong in Thailand, under the guise of transferring them to "health camps." According to diary accounts written at the time, the men were already deemed too sick to work, and were ferried onto the trains thinking they were being moved north to where there were greater food supplies, hammocks, gramophones, blankets, and mosquito nets.

But on arrival in Ban Pong, they were shocked by the realization that they had a 200-mile (322-kilometer) journey on foot ahead of them to Kanchanaburi, where they were put to work building a railway between Thailand and Burma. In the hope of invading India, the Japanese had seized on the ready-made labor force comprising British, Dutch, Australian, and American prisoners whom they drove with wire whips, bamboo rods, and beatings. In the most dreadful conditions the prisoners, along with civilian laborers, slaved for up to 18 hours a day, eating nothing more than a handful of rice and beans. Succumbing to cholera, beriberi, dysentery, dengue, and pneumonia, and suffering tropical ulcers that often led to fatal amputations, the men built a total of 258 miles (415 kilometers) of track—with one death for every sleeper laid, an estimated total of 113,000 deaths.

Now, a segment of the track connecting Bangkok Thonburi station to Nam Tok is still in use, with trains running three times a day in each direction. It is an extraordinary journey for passengers wanting to understand firsthand what the laborers had to endure. Made up of a rattling set of old carriages grouted together with rust, the train rolls into Thonburi station a little before 8:00 a.m.—much to the delight of nervous-looking passengers who can never be too sure that trains will run until they see them arrive.

Even though it should not take more than four hours to complete the journey, it is common for the train to break down at least a couple of times en route, so bring plenty of water and a fan to fend off insects. Once on the move again, you will soon find the light changing on board as jungle thickens on either side, and leaves and twigs thrash the →

→ windows, breaking off onto the floor. Creepers hang down, with heavy red blossoms falling all around the ground; and after monsoon rains the air is thick with the scent of wet mud from waterfalls tumbling into ravines.

Just before 11:00 a.m., the train reaches Kanchanaburi, now overrun with cafes, restaurants, bars, and shops selling tourist tat. Then, much to the delight of gathering onlookers, the train pauses for effect, sounds a bugle-like horn, and thumps onto the famous bridge on the River Kwai. Waving up at the windows, the crowd has waited patiently for this solemn sight, as have passengers who lean out of the carriage watching the warm river water twinkling in the sunshine. On the opposite banks, a floating village of thatched restaurants sways drunkenly around, strung together with rope and golden lights. In truth, the assumed River Kwai is not actually the River Kwai at all, but the Mae Klong River.

When he wrote *The Bridge on the River Kwai,* French author Pierre Boulle attributed the railroad to the wrong river. When fans of the book and David Lean's film arrived looking for it, the Thai authorities made a swift and smart decision to rename the river "Kwai Yai," meaning big Kwai, which satisfied tourists.

*A lovely element of Thai trains is the unbridled joy from the passengers, who you could be forgiven for thinking have never ridden on a train before. They kneel on seats, wave at villagers, and let out yelps of glee.*

Once on the other side, the train gallops on through fields before coming upon more rivers and precarious-looking viaducts. If you glance back from the front of the train you can watch the back carriages snaking around cliff faces, rumbling over wooden trestle bridges, and carving their way through wild jungle, so close that passengers often reach out to grab low branches. Here it is impossible to ignore the lives that were lost for the line's creation. Every jolt and screech of metal beneath your seat is a reminder that more than 100,000 people gave their lives for the train that you ride on now. So as you gaze out across the enormous river where floating hotels bob around by its banks, dense greenery falling into the water, take time to read about the history.

From Nam Tok station where the tracks taper off into overgrown grass, a short taxi ride will bring you to the Hellfire Pass Memorial Museum. In 1994, an Australian civil engineer named Rod Beattie began hacking through the jungle to uncover the old tracks that had disappeared under bamboo and creepers. Determined to create a memorial to those who had lost their lives, he managed to clear enough for visitors to be able to walk sections of track through the same oppressive surroundings, including through the infamous Konyu Cutting, also known as the Hellfire Pass. An enormous rock face, it was carved out by hand, using picks, shovels, hammers, and sticks of gelignite explosives lit by cigarettes. Beneath a canopy of greenery that keeps out the blistering sun, you can step over remnants of wooden sleepers, spikes, and rails that lead to a rocky pathway curling around the cliffs. The hum of mosquitoes is constant, the humidity draining, and the undergrowth sharp and thick enough to cut your skin. As twigs crack underfoot and sweat pours down your back, it is a pertinent reminder of what those prisoners endured many years ago, to build what is now a moving piece of history. ◆

Brought to Kanchanaburi under false pretenses, Japan's Allied Prisoners of War built a total of 258 miles (415 kilometers) of track—with one death for every sleeper laid, an estimated total of 113,000 deaths.

*Point of interest:*
the bridge on the River Kwai

*Make sure to:*
pick up a copy of The Railway Man
by Eric Lomax, an autobiography
about his experiences as a prisoner
of war on the railroad

From central Bangkok, a round-
trip to Kanchanaburi should
take no more than a full day,
but consider staying overnight
in order to explore the region
at a leisurely pace.

Sinakharin

Mae Klong

Chao Phraya

Hellfire
Pass

Erawan
National Park

NAM TOK

River Kwai
Bridge

KANCHANABURI

BANGKOK

MYANMAR

THAILAND

GULF OF
THAILAND

# The Reunification Express

*Running along the spine of Vietnam, a number of sleeper services connect the capital of Hanoi in the North with the megacity of Ho Chi Minh in the South.*

FROM HANOI TO HO CHI MINH CITY, VIETNAM
35 HOURS

The Reunification Express is not a single-named train, but a loose term for several services connecting Hanoi in the North with Ho Chi Minh City in the South. Once known as the Transindochinois line, the first segments of this 1,072-mile (1,725-kilometer) stretch of track were laid in 1899 by French colonists, and it was completed in 1936. The line was severed in 1954 when Vietnam was divided into North and South, and throughout the war the railroad's tracks, bridges, and tunnels were bruised and battered by American bombs. However, after the country's reunification in 1976, it resurrected itself and resumed a regular and popular service that allows travelers to trespass on the intimacies of Vietnamese life.

Over two nights, the Reunification Express meanders down the country, giving passengers the chance to see the effects of the country's history on its railroads, people, and countryside. At one end of the train, there are sleeper compartments with soft berths, curtains, and plastic flowers on the table, while at the other end there are sloshing toilets and wooden seats where passengers sit upright through the night, their necks at an angle, their feet on boxes tied with twine.

Whichever class you travel in, there is no shortage of activity, with children tearing up the aisles, raucous card games, and trolleys clattering through serving fried chicken and steamed rice. If you stand at the doorway, you will be able to see the engine boring into tunnels and curling around cliffs just as the South China Sea appears below in a magnificent burst of blue. ♦

The highlight of the journey lies between Hué and Da Nang where thick jungle surrounds the train as it runs above a creamy finger of sand called Lang Co Bay.

Passengers on an older train travel on wooden seats without the luxury of air-conditioning. However, one upside is that these carriages often have windows that open which makes for much better photography.

*Point of interest:*
*shuffle up to the window for the*
*first hour of the journey as the*
*train crawls through the guts of*
*Hanoi, offering a rare glimpse into*
*the intimacies of Vietnamese life*

*Make sure to:*
*break up the journey at Da Nang*
*and travel to Hoi An for a few days*

# The Darjeeling Himalayan Railway

*Lovingly known as the Toy Train, this narrow-gauge relic takes passengers from the Himalayan foothills to the cloudy heights of India's tea country.*

FROM NEW JALPAIGURI TO DARJEELING, INDIA
7 HOURS (2 HOURS FOR THE JOY TRAIN SERVICE)

Since the late nineteenth century, this sweet old steam train has been a much-loved sight on the ascent to Darjeeling. Puffing uphill like an elderly relative, it wails into view, black smoke trailing from its chimney. Trucks and carts slow to a halt to allow the train to crisscross Hill Cart Road, with amused walkers watching from the sidelines and gasping as the train runs so close to shop fronts that passengers could reach out and touch the fruit. Established by British colonizers, the railway was built to transport tea, rice, and other produce up and down the hillside. Now it takes big groups of Indian families singing Bollywood songs and is listed as a UNESCO World Heritage Site—one that the town's residents are keen to preserve. However, given that some of the locomotives were built in Glasgow more than 150 years ago, old parts are hard to come by. And as engineers die out, so too does their trade. Up until the last few years, the train departed from New Jalpaiguri and took more than seven hours to cover the 55-mile (88-kilometer) route. Zigzagging around thick bamboo and pine, it wound through emerald-green slopes of tea, arriving into the damp hill station where cloud hangs low like steam. It is unclear when the route might be resurrected, but for now, it is still possible to ride the two-hour "joy train" from Darjeeling down to Ghum and back, which includes entry to the train museum. On clear days, passengers should see the jagged head of Kanchenjunga dusted with snow. ♦

141

*Point of interest:*
the Batasia loop which
was designed to counter
a sharp descent

*Make sure to:*
pack plenty of food
and drink as there is
no service on board

Once used as a summer escape for the rampaging British Raj, the hill station of Darjeeling is now a popular holiday destination for Indian families and backpacking tourists.

143

# The Konkan Railway

*Opened as recently as 1998, this southwest coastal line is the most magnificent stretch along Indian Railways' 40,000 miles (65,000 kilometers) of track.*

FROM MUMBAI TO MADGAON, INDIA
12 HOURS 25 MINUTES

With the Western Ghats on one side and the Arabian Sea shifting quietly on the other, the Konkan Railway is a feat of engineering excellence. This 460-mile (741-kilometer) line between Mumbai and Mangalore is one of the only parts of the country's railway that the British dared not construct, leaving it to the ingenuity of Indian engineers to bore through some of the most treacherous landscape. Flash floods, landslides, and collapsed tunnels jeopardized many an attempt to extend the line, but in 1998, it was finally finished, and the first passenger train flagged off. Flanked by jungle, with the roar of water cascading down cliffs during the monsoon season, the route has fast become a national favorite. While a number of services pass this way, the best of the lot is the Mandovi Express, which takes just over 12 hours to travel between Mumbai CSMT and Madgaon in Goa. Setting off just after 7:00 a.m., the train passes through 92 tunnels and crosses 2,000 bridges, including the Panval Nadi Viaduct—one of the highest in India. With its doors flung wide open and warm air billowing through the windows, the train rolls by waterlogged paddies, mango trees, and miles of densely packed palms. Famed for its onboard pantry car, this train is a gourmand's delight. Throughout the day, hawkers wander the aisles with baskets of freshly fried pakoras, hot sticky chicken, and samosas. Passengers can walk down to watch chefs rolling dough for fresh chapatis, chopping chunks of fiery papaya, and tossing cauliflower in roaring karahis. Perched on a step with a cup of tea in hand, you will be able to see buffalo wallowing in rivers, children playing cricket with old planks, and endless sparkling ocean, before drawing into Goa at sunset. ♦

145

Point of interest:
the pantry car, which serves
the best food on the whole of
Indian Railways

Make sure to:
book a seat in 2AC class rather
than 1AC where you are confined
to a private cabin and will miss
all the action

A number of different services
cover the Konkan route, but the
national favorite is the Mandovi
Express which runs at a leisurely
pace, allowing passengers to
soak in the stunning scenery.

# Kandy to Badulla

*Trundle along clutching a cup of hot chai through Sri Lanka's tea plantations and misty mountains on the island nation's most scenic train ride.*

FROM KANDY TO BADULLA, SRI LANKA
7.5 HOURS

In the seventeenth and eighteenth centuries, Portuguese and Dutch colonial forces repeatedly tried and failed to conquer the ancient Sri Lankan kingdom of Kandy. The British only succeeded in 1818 by backing a coup. Visiting the mountain city today, it is easy to see why it remained an impenetrable fortress for so long: tucked into a meander in the Mahaweli River, it is protected by a circle of mountains. At first glance, it seems implausible that a train could wind through the green slopes without tumbling over the edge, but not only is it possible to travel down to Colombo on the coast, lines also run even higher across Sri Lanka's hilly heart. In fact, the whole purpose of building the railroad was to transport tea from the mountains down to Colombo. The train to Badulla is rickety rather than regal, but there is no questioning its authenticity, nor the sublime views offered across old Ceylon's tea country. Up here, it rains heavily and often, the smell of wet soil and leaves hanging in the air as the train shudders and clanks past waterfalls so abundant that the mountains seem to be perspiring. The British had originally wanted to use Sri Lanka to grow coffee, and initially, they were successful, but after disease devasted the crops in the late nineteenth century, botanists proposed a switch to tea. The effects of that decision are still visible today as the train passes above a sea of tea bushes, perfectly trimmed, with tea-pickers dotted in between. Even though the station in Kandy opened in 1867, it took until 1924 for the line to reach all the way to Badulla, a city defined by its still-booming tea industry. ♦

Trundling along at a leisurely pace, the train is often to be seen with passengers standing in the doorways, waving at friends, and basking in the warm sunshine.

152

*The train to Badulla is rickety rather than regal, but there is no questioning its authenticity, nor the sublime views offered across old Ceylon's tea country.*

*Point of interest:*
*Nine Arch Bridge between Ella and Demodara is an engineering marvel*

*Make sure to:*
*take a packed lunch and water; there may be some vendors on board, but do not rely on them to have everything you might need*

Keep your eyes peeled for groups of toque macaques bounding between the treetops. Endemic to Sri Lanka, these primates—known locally as *rilawa*—are easily recognizable by their golden brown coats and flat hairstyles.

# The Deccan Odyssey

*If you have ever wondered what it is like to travel like royalty, embark on this seven-night journey from India's capital to the metropolis of Mumbai.*

FROM DELHI TO MUMBAI, INDIA
8 DAYS, 7 NIGHTS

A royal-blue engine with gilded borders sails into the station. It heaves a sigh then comes to rest, pigeons fleeing from the rafters. Amid the sky-blue carriages of India's regular trains, this majestic character stands out, attracting curious onlookers who wander over to cup hands against its tinted windows. Not a soul emerges, then a door flings open and a red carpet rolls out like a tongue cooling off on the platform. This is the Deccan Odyssey, one of the younger members of Indian Railways' regal family of trains.

Much like its older sibling, the Palace on Wheels, this luxury service is a five-star hotel on rails. Offering a number of different itineraries, the train is a favorite with both Indian and foreign tourists hoping to tour the country from within the comfortable confines of air-conditioned suites, two dining cars—and even an onboard spa and gym. So if you have never ridden an exercise bike in the window of a moving train, now could be the time to try.

Each carriage is named after a region of Maharashtra, and houses private cabins fitted with soft beds, puffed-up pillows, and tightly stretched duvets adorned with a snip of pink hibiscus. "Welcome to a journey to the depths of your soul," reads a note on the pillow. A lucky few will travel in the grand presidential suites and can expect flat-screen TVs, a double bed, platters of fruit, and a personal butler who nips in and out to press laundry, bring tea, and leave gifts on the bed each night.

One of the routes on offer is the eight-day Indian Odyssey, which covers Ranthambore National Park, the Taj Mahal in Agra, Jaipur and Udaipur, pre-Mughal-era Vadodara, and the World Heritage Site of Ellora, before arriving in Mumbai. All passengers meet on the platform at Delhi's Safdarjung station from where the train travels overnight to Sawai Madhopur. Bleary-eyed, you will be given tea and biscuits and told to wrap up warm before disembarking to spot tigers in Ranthambore National Park.

Morning mists swirl around the carriage, and in the chill of the pre-dawn air, you are more likely to spot the beautiful creatures picking their way through the undergrowth before the sun warms the skies and the heat sends them into hiding. Jeeps grind gears and careen off at the slightest yelp of a chital deer—a warning of tigers—so keep your camera at the ready. Even if you do not manage to see a tiger, there are plenty of sambar deer, bouncing langur monkeys, and rare kingfishers perched in the trees.

*Bleary-eyed, you will be given tea and biscuits and told to wrap up warm before disembarking to spot tigers in Ranthambore National Park.*

Then it is back on board for a hearty breakfast, which could be poached eggs and sausages or *idlis*, *dosas*, and masala chickpeas with puris. If you are planning to take the train in the hope of sitting by a lace-curtained window with a crisp gin and tonic in hand watching a technicolor slideshow play out for hours, then you may be a little disappointed. For logistical reasons, and to save time, the train mostly travels at night. Over the loud crack of popadams, mounds of fluffy mutton biryani, and creamy raita, the train creaks and moves off, passengers far too engrossed in dinner and chitchat to notice. Once you are in bed, you will certainly feel the train snaking, and it is not unusual to have to leap out of bed to catch bottles of wine that jump off the desk and roll around the carpet.

But once the train has got into its stride, passengers will be rocked into slumber, waking in the morning to a brand new station. Throughout the week, you will be garlanded with sweet, wet marigolds, given many bindis, and entertained with dances, singing, and numerous other traditional shows. However, passengers are free to sit out excursions if it gets a bit too much; while the rest of the train disappears on a coach toward the Ellora Caves, or tours the pink city of Jaipur searching for pashminas and jewelry, it is perfectly fine to explore the surrounding area on foot or simply crack the spine of an old book and enjoy the peace on board. ◆

Point of interest:
seeing the Taj Mahal in all
its glory

Make sure to:
take a good pair of walking
shoes, loose clothing, and a hat
to protect you from the sun

160

From the moment you board the Deccan Odyssey, you will be garlanded with sweet, wet marigolds, offered many bindis, and entertained with dances, singing, and traditional performances.

*While the rest of the train disappears on a coach towards the Ellora Caves, or tours the pink city of Jaipur searching for pashminas and jewelry, it is perfectly fine to explore the surrounding area on foot or simply crack the spine of an old book and enjoy the peace on board.*

Cuisine on board the train is an experience in itself: expect silver thalis circled with tiny bowls of raita, masala potatoes, mutton curry, and dal, all served in two splendid cars.

PAKISTAN

Aravali
Hills

DELHI

JAIPUR        AGRA

SAWAI MADHOPUR

UDAIPUR

Ranthambore
National
Park

I  N  D  I  A

ARABIAN
SEA

AJANTA

ELLORA
CAVES

MUMBAI

# The Taste of Train Travel

*As your train winds through unknown lands, exploring the culinary offering on board can be just as exciting as the journey.*

One of the best aspects of train travel is discovering the food available on board, at the stations, and in the baskets of vendors hawking their wares up and down the aisles. On long journeys, it is the arrival or even the prospect of food that structures the day, with everything else fitting around it. But greater than the thrill of crunching into hot samosas on a Kolkata commuter train or slicing into plump scallops on The Ghan, is what these dishes and habits convey about a country's culture. For example, attendants on the Caledonian Sleeper rouse passengers with tea and a piece of shortbread, while Italian rail attendants bring espresso. Indian Railways serves cornflakes with hot milk—a colonial hangover—and in Russia, every dish is draped in dill.

If you find yourself roaming a Japanese station, you will notice bright displays of *ekiben*—a hybrid of *eki*, meaning station, and *bento* meaning lunchbox. Bound in bamboo or ceramic boxes, and tied with pretty bows, these gorgeous creations are unique to each station and made from local ingredients. Packed with rolls of rice, pearls of salmon roe, and ribbons of pink radish, they reflect Japan's unique brand of perfectionism.

On my own travels, I found that Chinese dining cars offered the best of communal dining, even if it was impossible to decipher the menu. With multiple passengers wedged in at tables strewn with chewed bones and cartoon-like fish skeletons, and glugging from small bottles of whiskey, the experience offered a fabulous insight into a people who take the greatest of pleasure in food. The roar of woks followed by great clouds of smoke that spread around the car signaled how fresh the dishes were, with trolleys of precooked food also coming up the aisles. Here, the best option is to point to what your neighbors are eating and hope for the best. Another tip is to have "beef," "chicken," or "vegetarian" written on a piece of paper in Chinese script to show to attendants as they come round.

The truth is that trains in Asia offer the freshest, highest-quality food that I have found around the world—at least on regular passenger trains. Thai dining cars offer set menus featuring duck curry, fried sea bass, steaming bowls of jasmine rice, and fresh pineapple for dessert—all for under $3. Indian Railways is famous for its onboard catering that is managed by one central company. For passengers unsure about what to buy when the train rolls into stations, play it safe and order anything that is deep-fried or cooked in front of you on high heat, especially if there is a long queue and local passengers are eating the same. Fried *dosas*, *uttapam* and dal-filled *kachoris* will all satisfy your hunger until the next hawker calls up the aisle with a tub of new goodies. On the newer, classier trains, you will be offered a tiny plastic tray with tomato soup, breadsticks, and packs of butter, followed by a new tray and a variety of foil-wrapped packages containing rice, tightly wrapped rotis, vegetable curry, and ice cream. Always carry a stack of small-note denominations as vendors are unlikely to be able to break large notes.

On the other side of the world, dining comes with its own charms: American mealtimes clamor with conversation between passengers who would usually never meet, revealing a universal need to connect and communicate across boundaries; and in Canada, you are sure to find a bison steak on your plate, while others dot the prairies outside your window. If you are uncertain about what to try, ask your neighbors, who will usually be happy to advise. But above all, be brave and get stuck in. ♦

A departure from South Africa's better-known luxury services, the Shosholoza Meyl trains are a more relaxed means of traveling between South Africa's Cape Town and Johannesburg.

# The Shosholoza Meyl

*Most travelers associate South Africa's railways with privately owned luxury services, but the country's long-distance passenger trains offer a safe, fun, and easy way to travel between cities.*

FROM JOHANNESBURG
TO CAPE TOWN, SOUTH AFRICA
26 HOURS

Punctuality is not a strong point of South Africa's trains. Arriving at Johannesburg Park station, passengers will invariably be told that the train is already delayed by a few hours owing to a sandstorm, an engine problem, or signal failures at various stations down the line. But do not let that put you off. While most travelers gravitate toward the luxury services that cruise between Pretoria and Cape Town, the Shosholoza Meyl trains are perfectly safe and enormous fun to ride, and they will not burn a hole in your pocket.

Pack a hefty book, some playing cards, and a box of travel Scrabble, and surrender yourself to the comings and goings on board. Offering two classes—tourist and premier—the train provides guests with plenty of options depending on your whims and fancies. Tourist Class sleeper cars have two-berth coupés and four-berth family compartments that convert to seating for daytime use, but be warned that there is no air-conditioning, so you are subject to the sound of wailing horns from passing trains and dust swooping in at night. Premier Classe is fully air-conditioned, and to the delight of most passengers who choose this option, has a buoyant dining car with jolly staff and four-course meals reminiscent of school lunches. Expect chicken Kiev, stewed meat, and plenty of boiled carrots, peas, and potatoes, along with lots of local wine. However, no one boards this train looking for Michelin-starred dining: here it is the scenery, the unsolicited conversation, and raucous games of spontaneous poker that give the journey its charm. From the windows, you will see hours of deserts and vineyards, sun-baked savannas, and deep red sunsets that set your face aglow. ◆

*Point of interest:*
*the dining car is the*
*hub of the action*

*Make sure to:*
*have no expectations;*
*you will arrive when*
*you arrive*

Be sure to pack a pair of
binoculars and keep your eyes
peeled for wildlife which is
always a bonus of traveling
through South Africa by train.

# Bulawayo to Victoria Falls

*Riding the overnight service from Zimbabwe's second largest city to the home of the world's largest sheet of falling water is the only way to make the journey.*

FROM BULAWAYO TO VICTORIA FALLS, ZIMBABWE
13.5 HOURS

"Do not do it." "Take a bus instead." "It is barely an hour's flight." For travelers lacking a spirit of adventure, the idea of taking the train from Bulawayo to Victoria Falls is madness, filling them with fears of packed carriages, grubby toilets, and constant delays. But that is just myth masquerading as reality. Built during colonial rule, Zimbabwe's rail network fell into a state of disrepair and dilapidation under former leader Robert Mugabe, drastically reducing its service. However, the country has since made investing in rail a priority, and while the trains are nowhere near perfect, they are now a vast improvement on what came before.

A lovely old building with huge potted plants, and wonky signs suspended from the rafters, Bulawayo station echoes with the clamor and shouts of passengers queuing up for tickets. It is impossible to book in advance, so turn up early enough to make sure you get a sleeper berth. You are unlikely to struggle, though, as most passengers travel in economy class, which accommodates 100 sitting passengers and their hand luggage. Only foreign tourists tend to opt for the comfort of private compartments and fresh linen.

Once you have bought your ticket, make sure to stock up on bottled water and some snacks in case the dining car is out of service, then make your way toward your carriage. Basic, with a pull-down sink, a sallow tube light, and a coat hanger or two on the wall, the accommodation is perfectly fine and clean for a 13-hour journey through which you will mostly be asleep. Do not be surprised if you find visitors peering into your compartment, curious to have a look at you and your luggage. More often than not, parents wander the aisles with bright-eyed children who will appreciate a smile and hello, and perhaps a nose at some photos on your phone.

With a hiss and a series of clanks, the train crawls out of the station past a graveyard of carriages, before rolling through trees already silhouetted against an indigo sky. Whether you travel in summer or winter, the sun still sets before 7:00 p.m., and the last shades of orange should just be visible on the horizon. From the open windows, you will be able to see mists draped over forests and speckles of yellow light from houses buried in between. As the train ascends to higher ground and the heat of the day disperses, it will feel chillier, so it is worth bringing a cotton sleeper sheet, a sweater and some socks to help you stay warm. Light sleepers may curse the horn which continues to sound on the approach to railroad crossings and villages, where those on foot observe and wave in amusement.

Despite the drum and clank of the train's snaking body, you will drift off, waking at first light to the sound of brakes squealing into Thomson Junction rail yard. Flanked by an expanse of mopane and baobab trees, the train is now running along the top of Hwange National Park, home to the big five safari animals, so stay close to the window as it is not uncommon to spot giraffes and monkeys roaming the savanna grasslands. If you have been lucky enough to avoid delays, some of which are caused by elephants strolling onto the tracks, the train should pull into Victoria Falls station around 9:00 a.m.

A calm, tree-lined space with taxi drivers roaming the platform looking for customers, the station is no more than a stone's throw from the zigzags of the Zambezi River, and a five-minute drive from the falls themselves. In 1855, explorer David Livingstone named the falls after the reigning British queen, but the indigenous Lozi people know it properly as Mosi-oa-Tunya, or "the smoke that thunders"—a more appropriate name for the mile-long mouth of the Zambezi River rushing over the edge of a cliff and crashing down 350 feet (107 meters) into a deep chasm. Visible for miles around, its mists colored by rainbows, the falls are an extraordinary sight and sound that roars in your ears, somehow wetting you no matter where you stand to watch. As the morning sun throws its beams at the spray, you will find this a more than conclusive and fitting end to your journcy. ◆

*Point of interest:*
*wildlife roaming the*
*savannas*

*Make sure to:*
*pack a flashlight as the*
*electricity can be a bit*
*temperamental on board*

Until 1905, when the railroad
from Bulawayo was completed,
the falls hardly received visitors.
Now, an average of one million
tourists visit the falls every year.

NAMIBIA

ZAMBIA

Zambezi River

VICTORIA FALLS

LIVINGSTONE

BOTSWANA

HWANGE
NATIONAL PARK

Lake Kariba

ZIMBABWE

Shangani River

BULAWAYO

# Rovos Rail

*Dubbed the Pride of Africa, this family-run luxury service was birthed from a pipe dream, but 30 years later it is still going strong.*

FROM PRETORIA TO DURBAN, SOUTH AFRICA
3 DAYS, 2 NIGHTS

Once upon a time, a railfan named Rohan Vos turned up at auction to buy a couple of coaches. His plan was to restore them and hitch them to an engine to be used as a family caravan, so he also sourced a 1938 locomotive from a scrapyard in Johannesburg. But it was not long before his hobby transformed into a business idea, and after hunting down more carriages, negotiating with South African Railways—and heaping pressure on his family life—Vos launched Rovos Rail in 1989.

Even today, every aspect of the luxury railroad has the warmth of a family-run venture, from the engines named after his children, to the way in which Vos welcomes passengers onto the platform at Pretoria—the origin of all six services. And what services they are: climbing aboard, passengers will smell the polished mahogany paneling and pressed linen. Excitement is tangible as guests wander the corridors, champagne in hand, peeking into bathrooms with standalone tubs, and leaning from wide-open windows. Reminiscent of Edwardian-era travel, the train's button-leather sofas, natty bedspreads, and etched-glass lampshades are more than pleasing to the eye, but that is just the start.

One of the most popular routes is the journey from Pretoria to Durban on the coast. Departing at 10:00 a.m., the train promptly sails out of the private station and bends southeast across the Highveld. With the skies burning blue and wisped with cloud, there is nothing more delicious than topping up your glass, turning your armchair to the window, and watching the grassy plateau fly by. Traveling on past goldfields and the province of Mpumalanga, the train gets into its stride, and belts along at a steady pace. Now is the time to wash up, look smart, and head to the observation car, which has an open-air balcony that is perfect for pre-lunch drinks, the warm wind whipping through your hair.

As you might guess, the onboard chefs serve up some of the most elegant dishes you will find on a train. From grilled scallops and rock lobster tails to ostrich fillet and traditional spicy beef bobotie,

the menu is packed with playful ingredients, while catering to all preferences. Needless to say, the wine pairings are sublime. After hot chocolate fondant or cumin-speckled cheese, push back the tasseled curtains and you should see the chain of Drakensberg mountains, whose prickly-looking peaks resemble a dragon's back—hence their name.

The rest of the day is fairly casual, with no pressure to be anywhere fast, so retire to your cabin and put your feet up. In keeping with the train's ethos, there are no radios or televisions on board, and passengers are encouraged not to use noisy devices anywhere that might annoy others. So stick to reading a good book or having a snooze.

Dinner is a formal affair, so make the most of the occasion and do not be afraid to glam up—but be mindful that the following morning is set to be an early one, so a good night's sleep is not a bad idea. As is normal with most safaris, it is wise to set off at dawn when the air is chilled and the animals are not hiding in the shade, so expect a wake-up call at around 5:30 a.m.

Today, passengers embark on a game drive around the Nambiti Reserve at KwaZulu-Natal. Driving around 23,000 acres (9,308 hectares) of private land, you have every chance of spotting the big five safari animals, along with cheetahs, giraffes, and plenty of birdlife. Fully committed to conservation and investing in the local community, Nambiti is also malaria-free, which means that passengers do not have to take medication before visiting.

The final day's journey begins with a more palatable breakfast time followed by a visit to the Ardmore ceramic art studio, where more than 60 Zulu and Zimbabwean artists create sculptures based on Zulu folklore and traditions, the sales of which support the Ardmore community and their families. Back on board, passengers can enjoy a long and leisurely lunch as the train barrels across the mind-blowing terrain of the Valley of a Thousand Hills, which looks much like it sounds, before arriving at Durban, the end of an incredible journey—but the start of a new one. ♦

*Point of interest:*
*a game drive in the*
*Nambiti Reserve*

*Make sure to:*
*bring a good camera with*
*you and plenty of memory*
*cards; mobile phones won't*
*do justice to the wildlife*
*and scenery*

The Drakensberg Mountains
were named by the Voortrekkers,
who thought the unbroken
chain of heavily weathered peaks
reminded them of the spines on
a dragon's back, hence the name
"Drakensberg" in Afrikaans.

With its big picture windows, comfortable sofas, and wingbacks, the lounge car offers passengers an area to mingle over a drink or a quiet corner to while away the journey with a book. On most days, afternoon tea is served at 4:30 p.m. in the lounge.

*As is normal with most safaris, it is wise to set off at dawn when the air is chilled and the animals are not hiding in the shade, so expect a wake-up call at around 5:30 a.m.*

Each train is made up of accommodation carriages, dining cars, a lounge car, a small gift shop, a smoking lounge, and an observation car with an open-air balcony. Maintaining the spirit of a bygone era, there are no radios or television sets on board.

*With the skies burning blue and wisped with cloud, there is nothing more delicious than topping up your glass, turning your armchair to the window, and watching the grassy plateau fly by.*

The Deluxe Suites accommodate one or two passengers in double or twin beds, and have their own lounge area and en suite bathroom with shower, toilet, and basin. A dedicated host is available at all times and services the suites daily.

# The Ghan

*Australia's most famous train cuts through the heart of the country, showcasing its indigenous history, flaming red landscapes, and fine wines.*

FROM ADELAIDE TO DARWIN, AUSTRALIA
53 HOURS

Kangaroos? Yes. Koalas? Of course. But did you know that the Australian outback is home to wild camels? They were imported to Australia from the Middle East, India, and Afghanistan to aid exploration of the arid landscape—it is estimated that around 20,000 camels arrived between 1870 and 1920. Able to travel for miles without water, the humped creatures were perfect for carrying heavy loads. However, these camels needed experienced handlers: migrant Afghans, or "Ghans," who played an often overlooked but pioneering role in Australia's history.

During an inaugural sleeper train service between Terowie and Oodnadatta in 1923, an Afghan passenger was the first to disembark at the little station of Quorn, where a crowd had gathered to inspect the new arrival. It is believed that as he sped off in search of a place to say his prayers, a railway worker joked that the train should be named the Afghan Express, which was later shortened to the Ghan.

After changing operators and extending its route from top to bottom, the train (which was once a much-needed commuter service) has now evolved into a luxury service enticing passengers from all over the world to witness Australia's landscapes from behind its curtained windows. Starting in Adelaide in the south, the train takes 53 hours to cut through the center of the continent, passing by the sloping Barunga and Hummock ranges and the whispering white turbines of Snowtown's wind farms.

The following morning you will witness dawn break over the desert in the outback town of Marla, before a bang-up brunch of gammon steak, fried eggs, and bubble and squeak. Then you travel on through a seemingly endless expanse of red rock to Alice Springs—the spirited, unofficial capital of the Red Centre—followed by Katherine, where you can explore the magnificence of Nitmiluk National Park, before terminating in the tropical city of Darwin.

Over two nights and three days, passengers will experience a little bit of everything Australia has to showcase, from bush towns, national parks, and indigenous townships to historic gorges, rainforests, sacred sites—and a camel or two if you look hard enough. Throughout the journey, there are options to include excursions in your itinerary, so take advantage of the fact that the train is burrowing into parts of the country that would otherwise be hard to reach, and that you might not visit again so easily.

Consider cruising down the Katherine River in Nitmiluk National Park, home to the indigenous Jawoyn people, owners of the area. Here you can view ancient rock art on sandstone cliffs, learn how the land plays a role in their beliefs, and birdwatch. But be careful not to disturb Bolung, the rainbow serpent, which, according to tradition, still lives in the icy depths of the green pools. There is also the option to embark on the spiritual trails at Simpsons Gap in the West MacDonnell Ranges, a short bus ride from Alice Springs. If you prefer to spend your leisure time on the train, however, there are still several opportunities to hop off for a glass of wine beneath the stars, warm your palms at fireside gatherings, and gaze in sweet silence at sunrises—so pack plenty of layers to stave off the desert chill.

Whether you choose to travel in Gold or Platinum class, you will have a private compartment and an attendant who will make up your bed during dinner, after which you can sway back up the corridor to bed while the train beats on through the night. With the focus on local suppliers, the train's chefs are careful about sourcing their ingredients and have created a menu that reflects the regions through which you will travel. While enjoying a pre-dinner tipple in the lounge car, you might notice the warm smell of saltwater barramundi being grilled, along with crocodile boudin blanc. Unlike a number of luxury services, the Ghan is not merely a magnet for wealthy retirees: expect to meet travelers of all ages and backgrounds sitting by the windows, including families and train-loving loners. On arrival in Darwin, there is a distinct feeling of having made it through a marathon—and in the best way possible, you probably have. ◆

*Point of interest:*
*Nitmiluk National Park,*
*home to the indigenous*
*Jawoyn people*

After working up an appetite
trudging around the outback,
you will be welcomed back
on board to dine on local
specialties that might include
grilled saltwater barramundi,
roasted kangaroo fillet, and
crocodile boudin blanc.

*Passengers will experience a little bit of everything Australia has to showcase, from bush towns, national parks, and indigenous townships to historic gorges, rainforests, sacred sites—and a camel or two if you look hard enough.*

Take a one-hour camel ride against the backdrop of the West MacDonnell Ranges, a signature Red Centre experience. From atop these gentle animals, you should be able to spot plenty of kangaroos, birds, and other native wildlife.

DARWIN

KATHERINE

Nitmiluk
National Park

ALICE SPRINGS

West MacDonnell
Ranges

MARLA

MANGURI

THE GHAN

Barunga
Range

Hummock
Range

ADELAIDE

AUSTRALIA

GREAT BARRIER REEF

BRISBANE

SYDNEY

MELBOURNE

PACIFIC
OCEAN

SOUTHERN
OCEAN

# Indian Pacific

*Named after the oceans at each end of its route, this Aussie classic carries passengers from coast to coast, passing goldmines, grapevines, and ghost towns in between.*

FROM SYDNEY TO PERTH, AUSTRALIA
3 DAYS, 4 NIGHTS

There is nothing like traveling across Australia to remind you how gargantuan and eternal the earth's landscapes are—with or without us in them. And while on board the Indian Pacific, passengers ascend into a meditative state as the silver train curls around fearsome rock formations, featureless deserts, and treeless plains that gallop into next week.

Just over 50 years ago, the first passenger train departed Sydney and pulled into Perth to the cheers of more than 10,000 people who had gathered to watch the arrival of the only train ever to complete an unbroken journey from coast to coast. Skeleton tracks had existed since the late nineteenth century, but passengers had to change onto at least five different trains to make the same journey. In 1912, construction began to fill in the gaps and build what is now the longest section of straight track in the world, from Port Augusta to Kalgoorlie. The 297-mile (478-kilometer) stretch has no curves, bends, or loops, and cuts straight through the heart of the Nullarbor Plain, whose name derives from the Latin meaning "no trees." And that is something passengers get used to on this extraordinary four-day journey across Australia's great outback, where tumbleweed is a more common sight than anything else.

Much like its sister train, The Ghan, the Indian Pacific is a comfortable and leisurely experience for those who want nothing more than to stare out of the window with no greater concern than which dress to wear to dinner. Usually traveling in pairs or big noisy groups, passengers have a choice of two levels of exemplary service with private en suite cabins, soft berths, and silky duvets—but that is where formalities end. The atmosphere on board is as one might expect on an Australian train: laid back, full of live music and good food. At mealtimes, passengers are steered toward the din of the Queen Adelaide dining car where the chefs prepare everything from grilled hiramasa kingfish and Hunter Valley tenderloin to blood orange meringue and sticky date pudding. Nothing is fried in oil and very few items are boiled to prevent accidents in the tiny galley as the train sways around, but do not assume that this will limit your culinary experience, which usually features local wines, honeys, and strong, rich cheeses.

Day one sees the train traverse the Blue Mountains, whose signature haze will be visible from your cabin window. The region's canyons and plateaus are covered in all varieties of eucalyptus trees, which release oils into the atmosphere and combine with water vapor and sunlight to create a rich hue. You will then travel overnight to the frontier mining town of Broken Hill, a nondescript little spot, but one of historical importance, where passengers disembark for the first off-train excursion, surrounded by flaming red earth.

The train plows on to Adelaide where it might be an idea to spend a few days exploring before hopping onto the next service that passes through, especially if you want to tour the historic wineries of Barossa Valley or simply check out the city at a leisurely pace. From there, the train takes an overnight journey to Nullarbor Plain, one of the driest regions in Australia. Scientists believe that more than five million years ago the plain was flush with trees and plants, but now it is little more than saltbush shrubland that invites you to wonder how life ever survived in this awe-inspiring expanse.

Later in the evening passengers are invited to disembark and dine under millions of stars at the tiny outpost station of Rawlinna, one of the largest sheep stations in the country. In winter months, passengers will get to share stories around a bonfire before returning to the train for the final night on board. Wake up to the smell of bacon and country-style sausages, and make your way to the dining car for one last hearty breakfast and chat with your companions in the lounge. If you have been lucky, this is usually when email addresses are swapped, and last drinks are clinked before the train pulls into Perth, an incredible 2,700 miles (4,345 kilometers) later. ◆

*Point of interest:*
the Barossa Valley

*Make sure to:*
bring enough layers
for chilly evenings

The Indian Pacific traverses
mountain ranges, arid deserts
and goldfields, rocky valleys,
and subtropical savannas on its
transcontinental crossing.

CORAL SEA

BROKEN
HILL

Blue
Mountains

ADELAIDE

Barossa
Valley

INDIAN PACIFIC

SYDNEY

MELBOURNE

TASMAN SEA

TASMANIA

# The TranzAlpine

*Take a sightseeing trip through New Zealand's rugged landscape, from the majestic Canterbury Plains to the backdrop of the mighty Southern Alps.*

FROM CHRISTCHURCH TO GREYMOUTH, NEW ZEALAND
5 HOURS

Such is the beauty to be seen along the TranzAlpine route on New Zealand's South Island, it seems incredible that the country does not offer more train services. Today, just two other long-distance lines exist, though when it comes to scenery, neither compares to the all-round experience of this 139-mile (223-kilometer) ride through the Southern Alps between Christchurch on the east coast and Greymouth on the Tasman Sea.

Owing to the rugged terrain and lack of public transport, most local people choose to drive, meaning this five-hour service exists primarily for sightseeing. And what sights: the might of these mountains inspired movie director Peter Jackson to film extended segments of his *The Lord of the Rings* trilogy nearby, the scenery offering such drama that he barely needed to add much in the way of CGI.

Deep in the Southern Alps, one of the optional stations is Arthur's Pass, a hub for adventurous hikers and one of the few remaining homes of the kea, the world's only alpine parrot. Like all six stops along the way, however, it is only made on request. While rare wildlife and glacial lakes do the work outside the train, those riding in Scenic Plus class have access to panoramic windows from which to take in the ice-blue rivers, beech forest, and glistening peaks, along with light meals paired with a long list of local wines. Rather than trying to hark back to a bygone era of train travel, the decor is sleek, modern, and functional, though none of this really matters when some of the Southern Hemisphere's grandest terrain is sailing past the window. ♦

209

*Point of interest:*
the Waimakariri River

*Make sure to:*
occasionally put your
camera away and soak
in the journey

The TranzAlpine Open-air Carriage has always been the perfect place for capturing views of New Zealand's scenery on camera. With redesigned carriages, it is now much easier to photograph the mountains and lakes without a patch of glass in between.

# Coastal Pacific

*Connecting the largest city on the South Island with the little port town of Picton, this train lets you soak up the sun, sea, and sand of New Zealand's East Coast.*

| FROM CHRISTCHURCH TO PICTON, NEW ZEALAND
| 5.5 HOURS

Few of the world's train lines have endured more tumult in the last decade than the northeast coastline on New Zealand's South Island. Powerful earthquakes in 2011 and 2016 caused extensive damage to the track, making it impossible for the Coastal Pacific to complete its five-and-a-half-hour journey north from Christchurch to Picton. Careful rebuilding and government assistance have helped bring the line back to life as a seasonal summer service in recent years. Like its sister train The TranzAlpine, which crosses the island from east to west, this service comprises modern carriages with panoramic views and offers menus drawing on New Zealand's extraordinary larder—not to mention its cellars. If you travel north, the colossal Pacific lies just to the right of the track for most of the journey— the ocean so close at times that you can smell the salt from the spray. The train twists and turns, offering a slideshow of farmsteads, towns, and beaches thrashed by the wind. In between glasses of Oyster Bay *pinot gris,* keep your eyes peeled for the glorious coastal town of Kaikōura. Located about halfway through the journey, it is well worth stopping off at for a couple of days. Owing to its unusual sea currents, Kaikōura is home to a population of ordinarily itinerant sperm whales, and you are guaranteed to see their tails flipping out of teal-green water with a backdrop of snow-covered mountains. Once the train has crossed into Marlborough, the landscape heats up to the ochres and yellows of dry grass, and its renowned vineyards whip by at a pace. On clear days, passengers might spot the distant coasts of the North Island before the train finally curves inland toward Picton. ♦

During hot summer months, the open-air viewing carriage is a great place to get some fresh air and enjoy the great outdoors while on the move. You can whittle away the hours chatting and gazing at the passing wildlife, beaches, and cliffs.

215

No matter how hard you try to bury your nose in a book, you will find distractions every few minutes as waves crash on the beach or whales blow spray into the air.

_Point of interest:_
on sunny days, the salinity in
Lake Grassmere can make it
appear a deep shade of fuchsia

_Make sure to:_
spend an afternoon visiting
the vineyards at Blenheim

# How to Pack for an Overnight Journey

*When it comes to packing, there is one golden rule to abide: the less you take, the less you need.*

It can be tempting to lay out pajamas, slippers, washcloths, face wipes, cleansers, chargers, books, pens, and diaries, but chances are you will not need even half of them. For an overnight journey, comfort is key. Cotton sweat pants are a good call, but beware of hemlines trailing along the ground, especially on trips to the toilet where the floor might not be the cleanest. Yoga pants that taper to the ankles are your best bet, with a loose top and a hoodie for when it gets cold. Even if you are on a train through muggy climates, it is likely that the air-conditioning on board will be cranked up high, so pack an extra sweater and a thick pair of socks: I was woefully under-equipped for an Amtrak ride between New Orleans and Los Angeles. Booked into coach class where the seats recline a little at night, I froze as a result of the Arctic-levels of air-conditioning, and proceeded to layer on the entire contents of my backpack, waking in Texas wearing gloves, a hat, and two pairs of socks. It then made sense as to why I had seen passengers boarding with carrier bags stuffed with quilts and pillows, with eye masks hanging around their necks.

Leave lace-up shoes at home and opt for a pair of slip-ons or sliders. The last thing you want is to have to fumble around in the darkness, retying laces every time you go for a wander. Most sleeper trains provide sheets, pillows, and a washcloth, so all you need is a silk sleeping bag liner which keeps you cool in the heat and warm in the cold. Folding into a small pouch, it will also protect you from insect bites. As for toiletries, a toothbrush with a cap will suffice—stocking up on hotel kits is useful for this—along with hand soap, toilet paper, and a pot of Vaseline for dryness, cuts, and scrapes.

But beware not to leave any of these things behind: before boarding the Qinghai-Tibet Railway, my husband discovered he had left his sneakers under the seat on a train now bound for Beijing. Horrified by the prospect of wearing flip-flops in the mountains, he ended up wearing socks inside his flip-flops, but was lucky enough to discover a shop selling the same brand of sneakers in Lhasa. Who knew? Ultimately, though, you need to keep your phone fully charged, load books onto an e-reader, lie back, and enjoy the ride. ♦

# Serra Verde Express

*Deep in the rainforests of Brazil, the Serra Verde Express is one of the only passenger trains in the country, corkscrewing around the jungle toward the coast.*

FROM CURITIBA TO MORRETES, BRAZIL
4 HOURS

So uncommon is passenger train travel in Brazil that the Serra Verde Express can feel like a mobile museum piece. The line from Curitiba to the Atlantic Coast was laid in the late-1800s as part of what was intended to be a more ambitious rail network across the South American giant. Those dreams were not realized before the advent of road and air travel, and today the line extends only as far as the historic town of Morretes, just 42 miles (67 kilometers) away.

Short though the Serra Verde Express's route may be, it takes a languid four hours to descend through the green rainforest which gives the train its name. Clouds drift through the tree-filled valleys, and as the altitude drops, you will feel the humidity dampen your skin. Passing through 14 tunnels and over 30 bridges, the train offers plenty of opportunity for passengers to lean out and spot howler monkeys and toucanets hiding in the leaves. Wet orchids sprout from the foliage, and post-monsoon you will hear the sound of water running down the slopes.

The track used to continue to Paranaguá on the coast, where Brazilian travelers often took a boat over to Ilha do Mel—Honey Island—but today the only people from Curitiba likely to be on the train will either be operating it or working as bilingual guides. Buses and ferries can help you complete the journey to the idyllic, car-free island, a place where the most complicated decision is choosing whether to have cachaça or rum delivered to your hammock. ♦

*Point of interest:*
the Carvalho Viaduct

*Make sure to:*
sit on the left for the
best views

Crawling along the jungled route,
the train provides passengers
with plenty of time and
opportunity to pace the aisles,
peer from the windows, and
absorb the lush surroundings.

*Passing through 14 tunnels and over 30 bridges, the train offers plenty of opportunity for passengers to lean out and spot howler monkeys and toucanets hiding in the leaves.*

One of the most memorable sections of this winding journey is where the Serra Verde Express enters the cloud forests of the Pico do Marumbi State Park before the sharp descent to Morretes.

# La Trochita

*Better known as the Old Patagonian Express, this legendary steam train still chugs through the desolate and windy wilds of the steppe.*

FROM ESQUEL TO NAHUEL PAN, ARGENTINA
3.5 HOURS

It is perhaps indicative of the state of Argentinian railroads that the storied Old Patagonian Express, known locally as La Trochita, now runs on only two selected routes for tourists. Yet La Trochita still represents something special. The most popular of the routes is the 12-mile (19-kilometer) stretch between the town of Esquel to the Mapuche settlement of Nahuel Pan. Built in 1922 to connect the foothills of the Andes mountains with the Atlantic Ocean, La Trochita got its name because of its 30-inch (75-centimeter) narrow gauge. Its service started over the decades but still operates using Baldwin steam engines first brought over from Europe and North America. With original wooden carriages clattering behind, the train attracts a number of rail enthusiasts, who flock to board the train made famous by writer Paul Theroux in his book *The Old Patagonian Express,* published in 1979. The sun-baked region is as notorious for its high winds as it is for snowcapped mountains and glacial lakes. Gusts often fly down from the Andes with such force that they can stop the train, literally, in its tracks. So do not be surprised if you are shooed off in haste. While you are on the move, snacks and drinks—including local specialties such as empanadas and *mate de coca*—are served in the bar on board, but the reason for riding is not for locomotive luxury, but to experience a slice of history. Anyone traveling this far into Argentina should also visit San Carlos de Bariloche, 150 miles (240 kilometers) north of La Trochita's terminus. One of the most beautiful towns anywhere in South America, it sits in the shadows of the Andes, among shimmering lakes, and is considered the outdoor capital of Patagonia. ♦

Point of interest:
a photo stop halfway
along the route

Make sure to:
keep small denominations
for purchasing local
handicrafts at the end
of the line

228

Passengers will be transported back in time while clattering along in wooden seats upholstered with worn leather, alongside a wood-burning Salamander stove in every carriage.

# Andean Explorer

*With wooden floors, fabric walls, and leather armchairs, South America's first luxury sleeper service is the coziest way to cross the Peruvian highlands.*

FROM AREQUIPA TO CUSCO, PERU
2 NIGHTS

Imagine waking up and raising the blind to see a Peruvian sunrise over Lake Titicaca. With a cup of coffee warming your hands, you can join other passengers outside in the cold or watch from under your duvet as the skies turn peach over water as still as glass. Many train journeys claim to be breathtaking, but few take that cliché as literally as Belmond's Andean Explorer, which ascends to altitudes that can make your head spin.

Starting the two-night journey in the buzzing city of Arequipa, the train travels overnight, arriving at the world's highest navigable lake at dawn, 12,500 feet (3,810 meters) above sea level. After breakfast, passengers take boats over the lake to the Uros and Taquile islands. The former are floating, man-made islands constructed hundreds of years ago from dried totora reeds that grow in the water. They are home to Indigenous people who live off sustainable fishing, potato farming, and tourism. The inhabitants of Taquile, meanwhile, are renowned for their colorful handwoven fabrics, which were recognized by UNESCO in 2005 as a "Masterpiece of the Oral and Intangible Heritage of Humanity."

In between excursions, there's time for unwinding in your compartment, sipping a pisco sour in the observation car, or chatting to other passengers in the piano bar car, with its wooden floors and splashes of bright cushions and throws, patterned with typical Peruvian stripes and zigzags. True to Belmond's levels of service, expect menus featuring seared sea bass, crisp duck breast, and puddings so pretty you could hang them on the wall. On the final afternoon, the train arrives in Cusco, the former capital of the Inca Empire. So rich is the region's history that it could take forever to explore, but almost all passengers continue to South America's most sensational archaeological site, mighty Machu Picchu. ◆

When the train is on the move, make your way to the lounge car and relax on gray tweed sofas with a freshly blended cocktail. This is the place to swap stories as a grand piano plays softly in the background.

231

The indigenous Uros people have
been living on the reed islands
for hundreds of years, where new
reeds must be constantly layered
on top of the old ones to replace
those that have dissolved into
the water.

_Point of interest:_
Raqch'i, an Inca
archaeological site

_Make sure to:_
stay hydrated to stave off the
effects of altitude sickness

*In between excursions, there's time for unwinding in your compartment, sipping a pisco sour in the observation carriage, or chatting to other passengers in the piano bar carriage.*

Having come this far, it would be crazy not to continue on to one of the most incredible archaeological sites in the world, the magical Machu Picchu.

*Starting the two-night journey in the buzzing city of Arequipa, the train travels overnight, arriving at the world's highest navigable lake at dawn, 12,500 feet (3,810 meters) above sea level.*

Building of the Basilica Cathedral of Arequipa began in 1540, the same year that the city was founded. Throughout its history, it has been destroyed by fire, earthquakes, and volcanic explosions, and was most recently restored in 2001.

# Chepe Express

*Enjoy the speedier, more luxurious way to see Mexico's rugged landscapes and mighty Copper Canyon.*

FROM LOS MOCHIS TO CHIHUAHUA, MEXICO
9 HOURS

First things first: there are two trains departing from Los Mochis, Mexico. There is El Chepe, the regular, regional service that travels to Chihuahua city, making 15 scheduled stops along the way—although unofficially it can stop more than 50 times. Then there is the Chepe Express, a fancy service with a bar on board that stops short in the town of Creel, from where passengers can take a bus to complete the journey to Chihuahua city. The former takes 16 hours and gives passengers a less sanitized and more lively view of Mexican life, while the latter offers a more comfortable option during its nine-hour journey time.

Whichever you choose, both trains allow passengers to hop off along the route, and to experience the same gorgeous views. Once the train sets off from Los Mochis, it squeezes between rock faces that almost skim the sides, blaring its horn to warn unsuspecting trekkers emerging up ahead. Circling rocky riverbeds and climbing to almost 8,000 feet (2,400 meters) in the Sierra Madre mountains, the Chepe Express makes its first stop in El Fuerte, a colorful colonial outpost that was once a thriving spot owing to its proximity to silver mines in the canyons. It is an ideal place to hike, fish, or try your hand at kayaking and rafting. Chugging onward, the carriages are shaded by tumbling forests one moment, then clattering across exposed, narrow ridges the next. If you make only one stop along the route, make sure it is at Divisadero. Here you can gaze out across the mighty Copper Canyon, which—at 25,000 square miles (65,000 square kilometers) in size—is four times larger than Arizona's Grand Canyon. ◆

Make sure to hop off at Divisadero. Here you can gaze out across the mighty Copper Canyon, which—at 25,000 square miles (65,000 square kilometers) in size—is four times larger than Arizona's Grand Canyon.

*Point of interest:*
Copper Canyon viewpoint
in Divisadero

*Make sure to:*
sit on the right side when
departing from Los Mochis
for the best views

# Coast Starlight

*Linking together the American West Coast's key cities, this spectacular Amtrak service takes passengers on a true ocean-view odyssey.*

FROM SEATTLE, WA TO LOS ANGELES, CA, U.S.
35 HOURS

Starting in the seaport city of Seattle, the Coast Starlight swings down the western edge of America, showcasing some of the best views, food, and conversation that Amtrak has to offer. While the first day's forests and valleys are pretty enough, the journey takes hold from the second morning when California shimmers into sight. With an iced tea or a chilled beer, take a seat in the sightseer lounge and look out across the Pacific Ocean where turquoise hues bleed into one another, and tiny waves peak in the blue. Students strum guitars, friends play cards, and solo travelers take notes, smiling to themselves as sunshine flashes through the carriage. Serving everything from shrimp in lobster sauce and enchiladas to vegan Cubano bowls, the dining car is where unlikely friendships are struck, as strangers sit across from one another breaking bread and swapping stories. Keep plenty of small banknotes and make sure to tip your attendant after each meal—15% is standard. At around 3:15 p.m., on the approach to San Luis Obispo, the train emerges from a tunnel and heads into the famously tight horseshoe curve before crossing the Stenner Creek Trestle. Move to the back of the train to get a full view of its body curling like a silver snake. From this point onward, keep to the right to watch the waves wash against the shore, white foam fizzing on golden sands. On the final stretch to L.A.'s Union Station the train passes small towns, evening surfers, and swooping birds taking advantage of the last light before a glorious orange sunset melts into the sea. ♦

# California Zephyr

*From Chicago to Emeryville, take a whistle-stop tour through the heart of America on board the country's most adventurous train.*

FROM CHICAGO, IL TO EMERYVILLE, CA, U.S.
51 HOURS

Traveling 2,438 miles (3,924 kilometers) through seven states, the California Zephyr is the longest train ride in America, clocking in at just over 51 hours. And what a glorious ride it is, cutting through the heart of untamed, timeless landscapes. Departing Chicago's Union Station three times a week, the Superliner service rumbles through Illinois before crossing over the Mississippi River into Iowa, taking almost four minutes to make the wide-mouthed crossing. Nebraska's golden prairies and flatlands slip by through the night, and you will probably wake just as the train is pulling into Denver, Colorado. As the smell of hot quesadillas drifts in from the dining car, you will feel the train begin its ascent into the Rocky Mountains, as evergreen forests drop away and red rock faces close in on all sides. Reserve an early seating for lunch, then take a crisp glass of wine into the panoramic sightseer lounge for a front-row view as the train curls into Colorado's canyons, rivers rolling and rushing below. Dipping in and out of pitch-black tunnels, the train plays a game of hide-and-seek with the sun before emerging alongside rapids that bounce lone kayakers along the river. By the early evening, you will cross into Utah, where the soft light ignites arid buttes and mesas into flaming towers of rock. Then the Zephyr moves on through Nevada and California, where it eventually swings around the Bay Area, past twinkling waters, before slowing into Emeryville, a short bus ride from San Francisco. ♦

Passengers are in for a treat on the California Zephyr: witness the might of the Sierra Nevada, feel the rage of the Colorado River, and marvel at the hues of Utah's deserts.

*Point of interest:*
the Donner Pass in the
Sierra Nevada

*Make sure to:*
book a roomette or bedroom
to experience the long ride
in comfort

# How to Stay Safe, Sane and Well-Occupied on a Long Journey

*Do not be shy! Riding the rails offers the rare opportunity to make lasting friendships—even if they only last for the duration of the time spent on board.*

You have found your seat, dug out your book, and had a good nose out of the window. But who is this? A stranger stops, looks at their ticket, then gives a tight-lipped smile as they squeeze past your legs. On a short hop, a polite nod and a "hi" would suffice, but what do you do when you are about to spend hours, maybe days, in this person's company? Unlike other forms of travel, taking trains is an intimate endeavor allowing you to intrude on the intimacies of other people's lives. When would you ordinarily lie in bed listening to a stranger grunt in their sleep, eavesdrop on chats between couples, or hold other people's babies on your lap?

The prospect of four nights on an overnight train can feel more than a little daunting, but oddly enough, short journeys are harder to weather. Much like being on an airplane, forward-facing passengers on regional train journeys sit upright in a tight space with nothing to stare at but the back of the seat in front. You might scroll through your phone, glance out of the window from time to time, and maybe stretch your legs to the cafe car and back, but there is little else to do.

Sleeper trains present a whole new world of fun, and they are a lot easier to endure than you might expect. Firstly, book an upper berth. During the day, lower berths convert to seats and universal etiquette dictates that you cannot stretch out and sleep. However, if you are in the upper berth you are free to sleep in, or climb up to nap and read whenever you please. Single women travelers may also feel safer in an upper berth, where you are much less exposed to passersby.

Make friends at the soonest opportunity, not just for your own pleasure, but in case you need someone to guard your luggage, assist with translating, or help you negotiate cultural nuances that may escape a foreigner. If you are worried about theft or drawing attention to yourself in cities where you are obviously not local, it is wise to wear a cloth purse on a long string around your neck that tucks inside your top, keeping your bank cards, passport, and cash safe from wandering hands and eyes. Keep anything of value in a smaller backpack behind your pillow or by your side under your blanket, and try not to draw attention to yourself by bringing out expensive cameras or laptops.

There are a number of ways to break the ice, but the easiest is to ask where your companion is traveling to. That way you can gauge how long you will be together and whether another character might enter your story when they leave. When traveling abroad, it is worth downloading a few translation apps that will help you navigate the journey, but another way to get chatting is to share food: offer around chips, cookies, or bags of dried nuts. If the scenery is particularly lovely or you see a monument or building you do not recognize, ask what it is.

On the other hand, some people may not want to chat (often in Europe), so take your cue from their body language. If their earphones are in, they do not look up from a book, or they refuse to make eye contact, they may just want some peace, so do not invade their space. However, having your own space invaded can result in lifelong friendships. While traveling through Canada, I met a wonderful woman named Karen who was traveling from Winnipeg in Manitoba to her daughter's wedding in Nice, France. She had vowed to stop flying and was planning on joining The Maple Leaf train in →

→ Toronto to New York, then setting sail on the Queen Mary 2 to Southampton in the U.K., from where she would board a train to London, take the Eurostar to Paris, and a TGV to Nice. She was one of the greatest inspirations and remains in touch today. In North Korea, I befriended an American veteran in his 80s named Bob who regularly travels to Mongolia, Iran, and Africa on his own, and he still sends me emails and photos of his travels. And on a hospital train in India, I met a photographer from Hackney in London who still travels the world with me today, photographing the journeys—including a few in this book.

If you are traveling alone, seek out the dining car. It is usually a hub of activity and a good spot to meet other solo travelers who might like to join you for onward journeys or share taxis at the other end. Otherwise, now is a good time to tackle

*War and Peace* or catch up with every series of *Game of Thrones:* download as much as you can in advance, as Wi-Fi on the trains is never good enough, and pack a pair of noise-canceling headphones—which could also help if you are on board a party carriage. Keep an eye mask, earplugs, and small denominations of local currency for snacks and bottles of water. At the end of your journey, you will feel an extraordinary recovery from cabin fever as you walk up the platform, stretching your legs, breathing fresh air, and knowing a hot shower probably awaits. ◆

Hovering in corridors, standing at windows, and buying a coffee from the dining car are good ways to strike up conversation and make friends on board.

# The Sunset Limited

*Traversing a diversity of landscapes, from the bayous of Louisiana to the Mexican border, the oldest named train in America is a real southern treat.*

FROM NEW ORLEANS, LA TO LOS ANGELES, CA, U.S.

45 HOURS

It is a myth that Americans do not take trains. While the majority might fly or drive from state to state, for the small remainder of the population, America's trains are a refuge. Filled with families, retirees, runaways, students, backpackers, teachers, tourists, military personnel, and those afraid of flying, the railways are the perfect place to encounter a cross section of American society—particularly on The Sunset Limited.

Departing three days a week, this beast of a train creaks out of New Orleans' Union Passenger Terminal, winding through the Big Easy before shaking loose the city and gathering pace across Louisiana, as it heads off toward California. Picking up and dropping off a colorful cast of characters along the way, the train takes just over two nights to cover the 1,995-mile (3,211-kilometer) journey to Los Angeles.

The oldest named train in America, The Sunset Limited first appeared in 1894 as a deluxe train that ran weekly between New Orleans and San Francisco. By 1913, it had become a daily service, but in 1942, the western terminal was pulled back to Los Angeles as a wartime measure. Once decked out in golden-age splendor, featuring double bedrooms and a French Quarter lounge where passengers smoked and drank gimlets, the train is now a pared-back version of its former self.

The Sunset Limited is a bi-level superliner service, with two floors of private accommodations per carriage. It offers passengers the choice of a roomette—a tight space for two with seats that fold into berths at night—or a bedroom, which has twice the space of a roomette along with a private toilet and shower.

An attendant will show you to your room, perform a turndown service, and be on hand throughout the journey, so be sure to tip them between $10 and $20 at the end of the journey. Passengers traveling in coach have upright seats with a decent recline: they are wide, spacious, and perfect for lounging in during the day, but at night you will need blankets, pillows, earplugs, and an eye mask to cut out the chatter and glare.

On the first morning, the train rolls through Louisiana's pretty little towns so slowly that it's easy to spot the curves on wrought-iron balconies hung with ferns, owners washing their trucks, and the flash of white columns on old plantation houses. Later, the journey takes you through sun-dappled bayous, and sugarcane and cornfields, with wooden churches hiding in between. After a long stop at Houston, a bell sounds for dinner when passengers are randomly assigned tables to set the world to rights over Caesar salad, flat-iron steak, and a glass or two of cabernet sauvignon.

There are seldom opportunities like this for the extremes of society to come face-to-face in such intimate settings, so make the most of the experience and do not shy away—most passengers are friendly, curious, and (if you are from overseas) will ask what you think of their president. If you are lucky enough to sleep as the train lurches through the night, you will wake to the Texan scrubland where lone horsemen kick up dust, jackrabbits spring about, and golden eagles soar overhead. It is a marvel to observe over coffee and a stack of hot pancakes.

While you read, doze, or eavesdrop on conversation, New Mexico's purple sage and giant cacti will flit past for a couple of hours before the train crosses into Arizona, where a phenomenal sunset awaits at Tucson. Here, passengers crowd at the windows with cameras and iPhones pressed against the glass, murmuring in awe as the skies burst into flames, the clouds ripple, and the mountains fade to blackness. It is a perfect homage to the train's name. By now, friendships have been established, books lie unread, and glasses are topped up with a congenial feeling of communal living. That is the beauty of American train travel: it is impossible to stay at the edges without being drawn into the fold. As addresses are shared, plates are wiped clean, and laughter drifts from the dining car, passengers sway up the aisles to bed, and the train barrels on through the night, pulling into Los Angeles just before dawn. ◆

*Make sure to:*
save some cash to pick up a
hot, foil-wrapped beef or bean
burrito from the famous
Burrito Lady on the platform
at El Paso

Tipping is a complex issue around
the world, where different countries
have different rules. On board
Amtrak, it is not unusual to tip staff
a couple of dollars each time they
serve you, although you can leave
them a larger tip at the end of the
journey instead.

259

NEBRASKA

IOWA

COLORADO

ILLINOIS

INDIANA

U S A

KANSAS

MISSOURI

KENTUCKY

ARKANSAS

TENNESSEE

TEXAS

MISSISSIPPI

LOUISIANA

HOUSTON

SAN ANTONIO

NEW ORLEANS

Río Grande

M E X I C O

G U L F   O F   M E X I C O

# The Skeena

*Winding west across the vast expanse of British Columbia to the Pacific Coast, this little-known train cuts through the heart of Canada's wilderness.*

FROM JASPER TO PRINCE RUPERT, CANADA
2 DAYS

Known for exceptional hiking trails, ski runs, watersports, and wildlife, Jasper National Park in Alberta is the first major stop for passengers arriving on The Canadian from Vancouver. While most disembark to play a few rounds of golf at the Fairmont Jasper Park Lodge or drive around looking for grizzly bears and moose, a handful of those in the know alight here to board the Skeena train up to Prince Rupert. In a country where few citizens use their own railroads, this commuter service has managed to keep a low profile. Unknown to the majority of Canadians, it is one of the most quietly spectacular journeys in the world. Departing Jasper three times a week, the Skeena—lovingly known by locals as the Rupert Rocket or its official name, Train 5—also serves as a lifeline to indigenous First Nations people who have no other means by which to travel across the least-densely populated area in North America.

Derived from the dialect of the Gitxsan First Nations people, meaning "river of the clouds," the Skeena takes two days to cover the 720-mile (1,160-kilometer) journey from Jasper to the Pacific Coast, with an obligatory overnight stop in the small town of Prince George. Until the mid-1990s, the Skeena operated as an overnight service running straight through to Prince Rupert, with sleeper berths on board. However, a downturn in the economy saw local communities suffer, and the mayors of towns along the route agreed that they needed business, so they concluded that the train had to halt overnight in Prince George. Passengers could then have dinner and find a motel for the night before reboarding the train in time for breakfast the following morning.

Between mid-June and the end of September, the train operates a "touring class" service, which includes three-course meals, complimentary wine, and wide, reclining seats housed in a domed panoramic viewing car. Passengers can also wander upstairs to another viewing level and look down upon the tracks, making it easier to spot wildlife. And what wildlife! From moose, caribou,

and mule deer to bald eagles, black bears, and grizzlies, this is one journey where you should keep your eyes peeled at all times. As the train eases out of Jasper, it is worth moving to the vestibule area in between carriages, where the top half of the doorway latches open like a stable door. Lean out and the wind will slap your face, drawing tears along your cheeks. Thousands of dandelion heads billow off the banks of the Fraser River, and the sweetness of pine is a tonic. When the weather is fine, the sun's rays scatter white diamonds across Moose Lake, whose shades of green billow like chiffon beneath the surface, and eagles scout the water for fish.

*While you are scouting for grizzlies, you will soon notice the aroma of roast beef in red wine drifting up the carriage, so make your way back to your seat and enjoy a three-course lunch provided by two jolly attendants in neckerchiefs.*

After passing the Cariboo mountain range, fetch yourself a cup of tea and move to the tail of the train before Mount Robson ascends into view: with bundles of cloud at the summit, the highest peak in the Canadian Rockies looks like a volcano venting steam. Against a burning blue sky, its crags and ridges flash and twinkle in the light, a glacier worming down its side like a vein.

While you are scouting for grizzlies, you will soon notice the aroma of roast beef in red wine drifting up the carriage, so make your way back to your seat and enjoy a three-course lunch provided by two jolly attendants in neckerchiefs. They are a dynamic double act who offer as many quips and comebacks as they do history and information about the surrounding areas, usually over a loudspeaker. With prompts from the drivers up ahead, they also notify passengers about families of moose and deer by the tracks. However, wildlife is not the only thing to stay alert to. Stopping at more than 30 stations between Jasper and →

→ Prince Rupert, with names such as Telkwa, Kitwanga, Kwinitsa, and Vanderhoof, the train draws out passengers you might not expect. Along with mushroom pickers, hikers, fishermen, and general hermits, they sometimes emerge from the woods to flag down the train—even if it is between stations.

With little to no public transport in the area, the train is one of the safest ways for women to travel across the province instead of hitchhiking along the highway that runs parallel to the track. Nicknamed the Highway of Tears, Highway 16 is synonymous with missing First Nations women, more than 50 of whom have vanished in the last 20 years. And as the lakes dry up, the mountains sink down, and forests rush to the trackside, it becomes clear how desolate this area is. The train stops at Penny, home to nine people and four dogs, its station no bigger than a country cottage. Then it is on to Longworth, a hamlet so remote that three times a week Walter the mailman opens up his house for two hours so people can come and collect their mail. For the rest of the day, the train rattles across historical bridges, traveling through First Nations reservations, past pulp mills and oil refineries before pulling into Prince George at dusk. Here there is not much to do but order pizza, take a hot shower, and sleep well before an early start.

*Thick forests of pine cover the mountainside and there is no shortage of lakes, glaciers, and rivers—including the Skeena, which the train follows all the way to its destination.*

The following morning passengers enjoy breakfast on board as the train continues with the second half of the journey. From the dome car, you will pass mile after mile of slim, trembling aspen that line the track, their round leaves shaking like tiny bells in the breeze. Thick forests of pine cover the mountainside and there is no shortage of lakes, glaciers, and rivers—including the Skeena,

which the train follows all the way to its destination. The train skirts canyons and crosses trestle bridges, and just as you start to wonder if the landmass will ever end, it begins to slow into the little port of Prince Rupert, a quaint spot famed for whale-watching and spotting grizzlies. Now you are here; spend a couple of days hiking the Butze Rapids Trail, eating hot buttery shrimp at Dolly's Fish Market, and sipping "cowpuccinos" on Cow Bay Road. It is unusual for passengers to ride the train back to Jasper, so consider taking the ferry down to Vancouver Island, which crosses some of the Pacific Ocean's most beautiful waters. ♦

Busy throughout the summer months, the train is also full in winter, with many passengers choosing to board on Christmas Day.

*Point of interest:*
Mount Robson, *the highest peak
in the Canadian Rockies*

*Make sure to:*
book your accommodation in
Prince George, where the train
makes an overnight stop

Read about the history of British
Columbia before traveling in
the region: First Nations people
have suffered greatly, and it is
important to learn their story.

PRINCE OF WALES ISLAND
BRITISH COLUMBIA
PRINCE RUPERT
HAIDA GWAII
CANADA
PACIFIC OCEAN
VANCOUVER ISLAND

# The Canadian

*Introduced in 1955, Canada's most famous passenger train runs from Vancouver in the West to Toronto in the East, covering nearly the full length of the country over four nights.*

FROM VANCOUVER TO TORONTO, CANADA
4 NIGHTS

Extending like a line of silver Dualit toasters from the 1950s, The Canadian gleams in the midafternoon light. The western terminus for this extraordinary cross-country service, Vancouver's Pacific Central Station, heaves with excitement as passengers mill around looking for carriages, waving to family, and taking photos in front of the engine. Beeping buggies sail up and down the platform transporting luggage, elderly travelers, and anyone else who wants to avoid the long walk to their carriage. Like a scene from the movies, attendants in blazers and highly shined shoes help passengers locate compartments and board the train, a hulking beast so high that it takes a step ladder to climb up. Once on board, it can feel like the first day at school with passengers wandering the aisles checking out each other's luggage, companions, and compartments, wondering who is traveling with them over the next four days.

Currently operating with two classes—economy and sleeper plus—the train attracts everyone from backpackers happy to sleep upright at night, to retired couples traveling in private compartments with bunk beds, en suite toilets, and shower access. Given the length of the journey, it is certainly more comfortable in sleeper plus, where you can enjoy proper rest, all-inclusive meals in the dining car, and access to the upstairs panorama car. As the train sails away from the station, passengers hardly have time to wash up before a call sounds out for dinner, and it is time to make your way up the swaying carriages toward the smell of beef pot roast and freshly baked bread. With a single rose at each table, white linen, and polished silverware, you might assume that entry to the dining car requires passengers to dress up for the occasion, but it is all very relaxed and perfectly acceptable to turn up wearing a fleece and hiking boots if you wish.

Here is where passengers have no choice but to strike up conversation, as the attendant will seat you together at random. You could find yourself across from an Australian couple en route to Toronto for their son's wedding, a Sri Lankan family celebrating a milestone birthday, or a group of golfers traveling to Jasper. And if nerves get the better of you, there is plenty of fine merlot on hand to loosen your tongue, not to mention the scenery sweeping by the window—always a strong talking point. By the end of dinner, the skies have darkened, and while the approaching mountains are still little more than saw-toothed silhouettes in the distance, there is already a clear sense of shaking off the city and galloping into the wild. At this point, it is a good idea to climb up to the panoramic car, where the night sky is sprayed with white stars.

The following morning, pull up the blind and brace yourself for a front-row view of the Canadian Rockies: easily the most beautiful stretch of the entire journey. Green lakes glitter at the foot of powder-dusted mountains, their heads aglow in the light. Fresh pine flushes the hillsides and waterfalls gurgle past the window. Before long, the train arrives at Jasper National Park where a number of passengers will disembark to play golf, spot wildlife, or explore the town. Resembling a ski village, downtown Jasper is home to grills, bakeries, and gift shops selling bear spray next to the chewing gum. Flower baskets brighten the streets, black bears forage in backyard bins, and taxi drivers will tell you how an angry elk once chased them up a fence. But all around are beautiful, sugarcoated mountains and hiking trails, so consider spending a bit of time here before boarding the train again.

From Jasper, the train continues through Saskatchewan's yellow prairies dotted with bison, past Manitoba's forests and Ontario's lakes, and ends its four-day journey in Toronto's Union Station. With the best of the scenery at the beginning and the end, most passengers use the time in between to read in the panorama car or congregate in the dining car over rich bison steak and plates of cheese. With plenty to do on board, it is easy to forget that this train is taking you across the second-largest country in the world, so make sure to look up once in a while and absorb the vastness speeding by. ♦

*Point of interest:*
the Rocky Mountains

*Make sure to:*
pack a pair of binoculars
to spot wildlife

As the train passes from one side
of the country to the other,
consider getting off at any of the
cities in between: Winnipeg,
Edmonton, Saskatoon, or Jasper.

*Pull up the blind and brace yourself for a front-row view of the Canadian Rockies: easily the most beautiful stretch of the entire journey. Green lakes glitter at the foot of powder-dusted mountains, their heads aglow in the light.*

Climb up to the Panorama car where
you will be seated by windows that
extend all the way up to the ceiling
and fill the space with natural light.
It is the most enchanting spot on the
train, both during the day and in
the darkness of night.

## Andean Explorer

PERU

belmond.com

*Courtesy of Belmond*
        pp. 231, 234 (bottom), 236

*Matt Crossick*
        pp. 232–233, 234 (top), 237

*Lars Stephan*
        p. 235


## Beijing to Shanghai

CHINA

china-railway.com.cn

*VCG/Getty Images*
        pp. 96–97

*Marc Sethi*
        p. 99

*Aerial Perspective Works/
Getty images*
        p. 100

*Jonathan Pozniak*
        pp. 101, 102 (top)

*Atlantide Phottravel/
Getty Images*
        p. 102 (bottom)


## Belmond Royal Scotsman

SCOTLAND

belmond.com

*Courtesy of Belmond*
        pp. 52–58


## Bernina Express

SWITZERLAND
TO ITALY

rhb.ch/en/home

*Alex Bozier*
        pp. 12–15


## Bulawayo to Victoria Falls

ZIMBABWE

nrz.co.zw

*Axel Bozier*
        pp. 170–171, 173,
        176 (top), 177

*Marcus Wilson-Smith/
Alamy Stock Photo*
        pp. 174–175

*Vasilis Tsikkinis photos/
Getty Images*
        p. 176 (bottom)


## California Zephyr

U.S.

amtrak.com

*Chris Mohs*
        pp. 247–248

*Lucy Laucht*
        p. 249


## Chepe Express

MEXICO

chepe.mx

*Catherine Sutherland*
        pp. 239–241


## Coast Starlight

U.S.

amtrak.com

*Chris Mohs*
        pp. 243–245


## Coastal Pacific

NEW ZEALAND

kiwirail.co.nz

*Courtesy of Great Journeys
of New Zealand*
        pp. 215–216

*tmyusof/Alamy Stock Photo*
        p. 217


## Eastern & Oriental Express

MALAYSIA TO THAILAND

belmond.com

*Courtesy of Belmond*
        pp. 123–124, 127

*Christopher Wise*
        pp. 125–126


## Indian Pacific

AUSTRALIA

journeybeyondrail.com.au

*Neville Marriner/Alamy Stock Photo*
        pp. 200–201

*incamerastock/Alamy Stock Photo*
        p. 203

*Neville Marriner/Alamy Stock Photo*
        p. 204 (top)

*Totajla/Getty Images*
        p. 204 (bottom)

*Neville Marriner/Alamy Stock Photo*
        p. 205


## Jazz Night Express

NETHERLANDS
TO GERMANY

jazznightexpress.nl

*Roland Huguenin*
        p. 27 (top)

*Joke Schot*
        pp. 27 (bottom), 28–29


## Kandy to Badulla

SRI LANKA

railway.gov.lk

*surangaw/Getty Images*
        pp. 150–151

*Julian Walter*
        pp. 152–154

*benitolinares/Getty Images*
        p. 155

## La Trochita

ARGENTINA

patagonia-argentina.com/en

*Jon Arnold Images Ltd/
Alamy Stock Photo*
p. 226

*Ezequiel Gonzalo Lopez*
p. 228

*robertharding/
Alamy Stock Photo*
p. 229 (top)

*imageBROKER/
Alamy Stock Photo*
p. 229 (bottom)

## Le Petit Train Jaune

FRANCE

sncf.com/en

*John Insull/Alamy Stock Photo*
p. 31

*Hilke Maunder/Alamy Stock Photo*
p. 32 (top)

*Chris Bosworth/Alamy Stock Photo*
p. 32 (bottom)

*Pierre Gillard*
p. 33

## North Korea by Train

NORTH KOREA

koryogroup.com

*Faruk Budak/Alamy Stock Photo*
pp. 106–107

*Austin Andrews*
pp. 109, 112, 113

*Ayesha Sitara*
pp. 111, 114 (bottom)

*Monisha Rajesh*
p. 114 (top)

## Qinghai-Tibet Railway

CHINA TO TIBET,
AUTONOMOUS REGION

chinatibettrain.com

*Jaris Ho/Getty Images*
pp. 86–87

*Jonathan Pozniak*
pp. 89, 91

*Marc Sethi*
pp. 92–93, 94 (top)

*Cancan Chu/Staff/Getty Images*
p. 94 (bottom)

## Rovos Rail

SOUTH AFRICA

rovos.com

*Courtesy of Rovos Railway*
pp. 180–181, 183, 184,
185 (top), 187

*Jurriaan Teulings*
pp. 185 (bottom),
188–189, 190 (top)

*Dookphoto*
p. 190 (bottom)

## Serra Verde Express

BRAZIL

serraverdeexpress.com.br

*Marco Sieber/Alamy Stock Photo*
p. 221

*AU Photos/Alamy Stock Photo*
p. 222

*Roberta Valerio*
pp. 223–225

## Seven Stars in Kyushu

JAPAN

jrkyushu.co.jp/english

*Jurriaan Teulings*
pp. 117 (top), 118–121

*Manabu Takahashi/Getty Images*
p. 117 (bottom)

## Shanghai Maglev

CHINA

*Paul Souders/Getty Images*
p. 105 (top)

*Marc Sethi*
p. 105 (bottom)

## Stockholm to Narvik

SWEDEN TO NORWAY

vy.no

*Emma Wood/Alamy Stock Photo*
p. 22 (top)

*Arctic Photo/Alamy Stock Photo*
p. 22 (bottom)

*anjci/Getty Images*
pp. 24–25

## The Caledonian Sleeper

ENGLAND TO SCOTLAND

sleeper.scot

*Michael Turek*
p. 47

## The Canadian

CANADA

viarail.ca/en

*Courtesy of VIA Rail Extranet*
pp. 272–281

## The Cinque Terre Railway

ITALY

trenitalia.com

*Julia Lavrinenko/Alamy Stock Photo*
p. 37

*nycshooter/Getty Images*
pp. 38–39

*Christian Müller/Alamy Stock Photo*
p. 40

*Axel Bozier*
p. 41 (top)

*Ana Tramont/Getty Images*
p. 41 (bottom)

## The Darjeeling Himalayan Railway

INDIA

indianrail.gov.in

*xPACIFICA/Getty Images*
pp. 140–141

*Annapurna Mellor*
pp. 142, 143 (top)

*Pavliha/Getty Images*
p. 143 (bottom)

## The Death Railway

THAILAND

railway.co.th

*banjongseal324/Getty Images*
pp. 128–129

*Annapurna Mellor*
pp. 131–134

## The Deccan Odyssey

INDIA

indianrailways.gov.in

*ferrantraite/Getty Images*
pp. 156–157

*Courtesy of Deccan Odyssey*
pp. 159–162

*hadynyah/Getty Images*
p. 163

## The Douro Valley Railway

PORTUGAL

cp.pt/passageiros/pt

*Georg Trüb*
pp. 42–45

## The French Riviera Railway

FRANCE TO ITALY

sncf.com/en

*John Lamb/Getty Images*
p. 34

## The Ghan

AUSTRALIA

journeybeyondrail.com.au

*Rhiannon Taylor*
pp. 192–197, 198 (bottom)

*Scott A. Woodward*
p. 198 (top)

## The Golden Eagle

KAZAKHSTAN
TO RUSSIA

goldeneagleluxurytrains.com

*Jurriaan Teulings*
pp. 83–85

## The Konkan Railway

INDIA

indianrailways.gov.in

*Dinodia Photo/Getty Images*
pp. 144–145

*Lalam Mandavkar*
pp. 146 (bottom), 147

*Anders Blomqvist/Getty Images*
p. 146 (top)

*Raphael Sammut/Getty Images*
pp. 148–149

## The Rauma Railway

NORWAY

sj.no

*Maarten van der Velden*
pp. 16, 21

*CHROMORANGE/Alamy Stock Photo*
p. 18 (top)

*Ian Bottle/Alamy Stock Photo*
p. 18 (bottom)

*Geoff Shaw/Alamy Stock Photo*
p. 19

## The Reunification Express

VIETNAM

vietnam-railway.com

*Ismael Monfort Vialcanet/Alamy Stock Photo*
pp. 137–138

*Lars Stephan*
p. 139

## The Shosholoza Meyl

SOUTH AFRICA

shosholozameyl.co.za

*ITPhoto/Alamy Stock Photo*
p. 166 (top)

*Pete Titmuss/Alamy Stock Photo*
p. 166 (bottom)

*Greg Balfour Evans/Alamy Stock Photo*
p. 168 (top)

*Jacintha Verdegaal*
pp. 168 (bottom), 169

## The Skeena

CANADA

viarail.ca

*Courtesy of VIA Rail Extranet*
pp. 262–263, 267, 269

*Michael Heinisch/Alamy Stock Photo*
p. 265

*VW Pics/Getty Images*
p. 268

## The Sunset Limited

U.S.

amtrak.com

*Sean Pavone/Alamy Stock Photo*
pp. 254–255

*Rachael Wright*
p. 258

*Sally Mundy/Alamy Stock Photo*
p. 257

*Brian Welker/Alamy Stock Photo*
p. 259 (top)

*halbergman/Getty Images*
p. 259 (bottom)

# Epic Train Journeys

*The Inside Track to the
World's Greatest Rail Routes*

*Monisha Rajesh*

This book was conceived, edited, and
designed by *gestalten*.

Written by *Monisha Rajesh*
Copy edited by *Michael Haydock*

Edited by *Robert Klanten* and *Elli Stuhler*
Contributing Editor: *Monisha Rajesh*

Editorial Management by *Anna Diekmann*
Photo Editor: *Valentina Marinai*

Cover, Design, and Layout by *Stefan Morgner*
Head of Design: *Niklas Juli*
Illustrations by *Martin Haake*

Typefaces: Freight Text by *Joshua Darden*

Cover image courtesy of *Via Rail Canada*
Backcover image by *Axel Bozier*

Printed by *Printer Trento s. r. l., Trento, Italy*
Made in Europe

Published by gestalten, Berlin 2021
ISBN 978-3-96704-020-3

For more information, and to order books,
please visit www.gestalten.com

Bibliographic information published by the Deutsche
Nationalbibliothek. The Deutsche Nationalbibliothek
lists this publication in the Deutsche Nationalbibliografie;
detailed bibliographic data is available online at
www.dnb.de

None of the content in this book was published in
exchange for payment by commercial parties or
designers; gestalten selected all included work based
solely on its artistic merit.

This book was printed on paper certified according
to the standards of the FSC®.

MONISHA RAJESH is an author and journalist who has
worked for the likes of *Time*, *Vanity Fair*, *The New York
Times*, and *The Guardian*. She was also a train travel
columnist for *The Sunday Telegraph*. Her first book,
*Around India in 80 Trains* (2012) was featured in *The
Independent*'s top ten books on India. Her second book,
*Around the World in 80 Trains* (2019) won the *National
Geographic Travel Book of The Year* prize and was short-
listed for the *Stanford Dolman Award*.